Also by Lorraine Bodger

✳

Great American Cookies
Great American Cakes
The Christmas Kitchen
Chicken Dinners
The Complete Vegetable Cookbook
Savory Tarts
Chutneys and Relishes
Sweet and Savory Sauces
Chocolate Cookies

A Year of Cookies

52 Recipes for Everyday and Holiday Cookies to Bake and Enjoy Year-Round

Written and illustrated by Lorraine Bodger

St. Martin's Griffin ❧ New York

Design by Ellen R. Sasahara

Library of Congress Cataloging-in-Publication Data

Bodger, Lorraine.
    A year of cookies : 52 recipes for everyday and holiday cookies to bake and enjoy year-round / Lorraine Bodger ; illustrations by Lorraine Bodger. — 1st ed.
        p.   cm.
    ISBN 0-312-19964-3
    1. Cookies. I. Title.
TX772.B6324   1999
641.8'654—dc21   98-37528
                                                                                         CIP

First St. Martin's Griffin Edition: January 1999

10 9 8 7 6 5 4 3 2 1

Contents

A Year of Cookies

Making Cookies

WINTER, SPRING, SUMMER, AND FALL—homemade cookies are one of life's small but perfect delights, easily available to anyone with a sweet tooth and an hour to spare. If you're an experienced baker, you'll be familiar with most of the following suggestions and guidelines; if you're new to cookie baking, everything you need to know is right here.

- Read the entire recipe before you begin baking.
- Don't skimp on ingredients; use the best quality you can afford.
- Unless otherwise specified, use unsalted (sweet) butter, all-purpose flour, white granulated sugar, large eggs, and ground spices. If the recipe calls for nuts, taste them before adding; nuts must be absolutely fresh, not stale or rancid. Dried fruit, raisins, and currants should be soft. Always use pure vanilla extract—no imitations. Never use chocolate-flavored products, either; if possible, buy high-quality chocolate such as Callebaut, Lindt, Valrhona, or Ghirardelli. When cocoa powder is listed in the ingredients, use pure, unsweetened cocoa powder, not cocoa mix.
- In these recipes, there's no need to sift flour before measuring it.
- Measure ingredients carefully. For liquids, use clear glass or plastic

measuring cups; for dry ingredients, use metal cups or measuring spoons that can be leveled off with a knife or spatula.

•To measure dry ingredients (flour, granulated sugar, confectioners' sugar, cocoa, baking powder or baking soda, spices), spoon into a measuring cup or measuring spoon and level off. To measure light or dark brown sugar, pack it so firmly into a metal measuring cup that it holds its shape when turned out.

•Use shiny—not dark—baking sheets (also called cookie sheets) that fit on the oven rack with at least two inches between each edge of the baking sheet and the adjacent wall of the oven; this allows the heat to circulate freely. Have two baking sheets available—one to go in the oven while you prepare the second. If you need extras, use jelly roll pans or inverted baking pans.

•Cookies should be baked in the center of the oven, so shift one oven rack to the center slot.

•Preheat the oven for 10 to 15 minutes. Be sure your oven temperature is correct; if it isn't, the baking times given in the recipes won't be reliable. For more information on checking your oven temperature, see page 6.

•To grease and flour a baking sheet, first apply a thin coat of soft butter or margarine to the baking sheet; a pastry brush works well for this job. Then sprinkle the greased sheet with flour and (working over the sink) tap it briskly while you tilt it back and forth. Tip excess flour into the sink.

•Use an electric mixer for creaming butter and sugar; beat until the sugar is barely grainy. This can take a few minutes, so be patient.

•Set your kitchen timer when you put a sheet of cookies into the oven. The baking times in the recipes have been carefully tested, so if one baking time is given (for example, 11 minutes), set your timer for that number. If a choice of times is given in the recipe (for example, 8 to 10 minutes), set the timer for the lower number and check the cookies when the timer goes off. If the cookies are done, as described in the recipe, remove the baking sheet from the oven; if not, continue baking for the additional number of minutes.

• When making batches of cookies, it's not necessary to wash each baking sheet every time you reuse it. Instead, just scrape off crumbs and wipe with a paper towel. Be sure the baking sheet is cool before you grease it again or put more cookie dough on it.

• When cookies are done, let them cool as instructed in the recipe. Loosen them all at the same time with a metal spatula or pancake turner and transfer to wire racks, making a single layer of cookies. Be sure cookies are completely cool before you stack them or store them. (You'll find cookie storage information on page 6.)

• If your baked cookies cool too long on the baking sheet and become stuck, return the sheet to the oven for a minute or so; they should loosen up. Remove and let them cool as usual.

BAKER'S BATTERIE DE CUISINE

Much of this equipment is already on your kitchen shelves, and some of it you may wish to add in order to enjoy cookie baking even more.

Basics
• Graduated measuring cups (dry ingredients); glass or plastic measuring cup (liquid ingredients)
• Measuring spoons
• Small and large mixing bowls

- Heavy saucepan for melting butter or chocolate
- Box grater for making grated lemon or orange rind
- Wooden spoons for mixing by hand
- Wire whisk
- Electric mixer with variable speeds (handheld is fine)
- Rubber spatulas for scraping down the bowls
- Rolling pin
- Oven thermometer (mercury type)
- Timer
- Baking sheets (shiny, not dark)
- Jelly roll pan (for bar cookies; as an extra baking sheet)
- Baking pans in standard sizes for bar cookies (see recipes for exact measurements)
- Metal spatula or pancake turner for removing cookies from the baking sheet
- Wire racks for cooling the cookies

Nonessential, but nice to have
- Gel food coloring
- Wide and narrow pastry brushes
- Gem muffin pans, for making tartlets
- Assorted cookie cutters
- Cookie press with a variety of disks
- Pastry bag with a few large and small tips
- Food processor
- Kitchen scale

BAKER'S PANTRY

You won't need all these supplies for every cookie recipe, but you'll want to have all the basics on hand, as well as many of the other ingredients.

Basics
- Flour (all-purpose)
- Baking powder; baking soda
- Salt
- Sugar (white granulated)
- Unsalted butter
- Eggs (large)
- Pure vanilla extract

Other Ingredients
- Superfine sugar
- Light brown sugar; dark brown sugar
- Confectioners' sugar (also called powdered sugar)
- Other sweeteners: honey, molasses, light corn syrup
- Margarine
- Nuts: walnuts, pecans, almonds, hazelnuts, pine nuts, pistachios, macadamias, peanuts
- Almond extract
- Pure almond paste
- Chocolate (in blocks or chunks): unsweetened, semisweet
- Semisweet chocolate chips (regular, miniature)

- Cocoa powder
- Raisins, currants
- Sweetened shredded coconut
- Ground spices: cinnamon, ginger, nutmeg, allspice, cloves

KNOW YOUR OVEN

If your oven doesn't heat to the right temperature, your cookies won't bake properly in the specified baking time. But how can you be sure your oven temperature is correct? By testing it with an oven thermometer. Here's how: Put a mercury-type oven thermometer in the middle of an oven rack placed in the center slot of the oven. Preheat for 15 minutes and then check the thermometer. If the temperature setting disagrees with the reading on the thermometer, adjust the setting up or down accordingly.

COOKIE STORAGE

Basics: Keep cookies with distinctive flavors (such as spice, chocolate, or peanut butter) in separate containers so the flavors don't mix. Never store soft cookies and crisp cookies in the same container. (Cookies that become a little too soft can be crisped or freshened by heating them in a 325°F oven for 1 or 2 minutes.)

Containers: Cookie jars, glass jars, or plastic containers with close-fitting lids are excellent for protecting your cookies and keeping them fresh. So are zip-lock-type plastic bags, although cookies in plastic bags may, of course, break or crumble.

Freezing: Most cookies freeze well in zip-lock bags or in airtight plastic containers. Bar cookies should be wrapped snugly in plastic wrap (in packets of four, eight, or any other family-friendly amount), then sealed in zip-lock bags or plastic containers. To defrost, spread cookies in a single layer on a wire rack and let them come to room temperature. If necessary, crisp the cookies in a 325°F oven for a minute or two; let them cool before serving.

January

IT'S COLD AND SNOWY OUTSIDE, snug and cozy inside—January is the perfect month to spend time baking cookies in your warm kitchen. Keep the cookie jar filled with crisp Iced Molasses Drops, rich Double-Chocolate Shortbread, crunchy Swedish Almond Toast, or tender Pecan–Cream Cheese Cookies.

ICED MOLASSES DROPS

Makes about 3 ¹/₂ dozen cookies

Thin and crisp, not too spicy, with a light molasses flavor. The vanilla icing gives the cookies a lovely finish (especially nice for guests), but it's not essential.

1½ cups flour
¾ teaspoon baking soda
¼ teaspoon salt
¼ teaspoon cinnamon
¼ teaspoon ground ginger
½ cup (1 stick) unsalted butter, at
   room temperature
¾ cup packed light brown sugar
3 tablespoons unsulphured molasses
   (not blackstrap)
1 egg

For the icing (optional):
1 tablespoon unsalted butter,
   melted
¾ teaspoon vanilla extract
2 tablespoons milk
Pinch of salt
1 cup sifted confectioners' sugar

1. Preheat the oven to 350°F; grease 1 or 2 baking sheets. In a small bowl, stir or whisk together the flour, baking soda, salt, and spices.
2. In a large bowl, cream the butter and brown sugar. Gradually add the molasses, blending well after each addition. Add the egg and beat again. Gradually add the flour mixture, blending well after each addition.
3. Drop the dough by rounded teaspoons, 2 inches apart, onto the pre-

pared baking sheet. Use a flour-dipped fork to flatten each drop slightly.

4. Bake for 10 to 12 minutes, until the cookies are a rich brown; do not let the edges burn. Transfer immediately to wire racks to cool.

5. Make the icing, if using: Stir together the melted butter, vanilla, milk, and salt. Add the confectioners' sugar and beat until smooth. This icing sets quickly, so if you're not going to use it immediately, cover it with plastic wrap pressed directly onto the surface of the icing.

6. Top each cookie with about $\frac{1}{2}$ teaspoon of icing and spread with a small spatula. Leave the iced cookies on waxed paper or wire racks until the icing is firm.

DOUBLE-CHOCOLATE SHORTBREAD

Makes about 56 bars

Intensely chocolaty, crisp and buttery—wicked is the only word for this short-bread. Try not to eat all the cookies at once; wrap some of them snugly in plastic and freeze for another day.

1¾ cups flour
½ cup cocoa powder, sifted
¼ teaspoon salt
1 cup (2 sticks) unsalted butter, at room temperature
½ cup superfine sugar
1 teaspoon vanilla extract
1 cup chopped high-quality semisweet chocolate (such as Callebaut, Lindt, Valrhona, or Ghirardelli), *or* 1 cup miniature chocolate chips

1. In a small bowl, stir or whisk together the flour, cocoa, and salt.
2. In a large bowl, cream the butter, sugar, and vanilla. Gradually add the flour mixture, blending well after each addition. Stir in the chopped chocolate (or the chocolate chips).
3. Carefully divide the dough in half and place each piece on an ungreased baking sheet. With moistened hands, pat out each piece to a rectangle 4 inches wide and ¼ inch thick; use a ruler for correct measure-

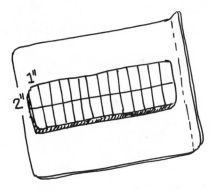

ments. Using the edge of the ruler, deeply score (but *do not cut*) each rectangle in 1 × 2-inch bars, as shown. Use a fork to prick each wedge 3 or 4 times. Cover with plastic wrap and refrigerate for 1 hour, or until firm.

4. Preheat the oven to 325°F. Cut the chilled dough into bars, following the scored lines, and use a spatula to place them 1 inch apart on the baking sheets.

5. If you have time, bake 1 sheet at a time in the center of the oven for 30 minutes, until the bars are firm to the touch and crisp at the edges; be careful not to let them burn. If you prefer, bake both sheets at the same time, 1 sheet on the middle shelf and 1 on the shelf above, for 20 minutes; then reverse the positions of the baking sheets in the oven and bake for about 10 minutes longer. Let the bars cool on the baking sheet for 2 or 3 minutes, then carefully transfer to wire racks to finish cooling.

SWEDISH ALMOND TOAST

Makes about 20 slices

These light, toasted slices are crunchy and mildly sweet—completely satisfying when you want a little treat that isn't quite like dessert. Easy to make, too.

1½ cups plus 1 tablespoon flour
½ teaspoon baking powder
¼ teaspoon baking soda
⅛ teaspoon salt
½ cup (1 stick) unsalted butter, at room
   temperature
½ cup sugar
1 egg
1½ tablespoons sour cream
½ teaspoon vanilla extract
½ teaspoon almond extract
½ cup finely chopped blanched almonds

1. Preheat the oven to 350°F; grease 1 baking sheet and have ready 1 or 2 ungreased baking sheets. In a small bowl, stir or whisk together 1½ cups of the flour and the baking powder, baking soda, and salt.

2. In a large bowl, cream the butter and sugar. Add the egg, sour cream, vanilla, and almond extract and beat well. Gradually add the flour mixture, blending just until mixed. Stir in the almonds. Sprinkle with the

remaining tablespoon of flour and stir again. Turn out the dough onto a flour-dusted surface and knead lightly 10 times.

3. Place the dough on the greased baking sheet and shape it into a log about 1½ inches in diameter. Flatten slightly.

4. Bake for 30 minutes, until lightly colored and fairly firm. Remove from the oven and reduce the oven temperature to 250°F.

5. Use a serrated knife to cut the log in ½-inch slices; at this stage the dough is crumbly, so cut carefully. Lay the slices flat on the ungreased baking sheet.

6. Bake for 20 minutes longer, until the bottoms are lightly toasted. Turn the slices over and bake for 20 minutes more. Transfer the cookies to wire racks to cool.

PECAN–CREAM CHEESE COOKIES

Makes 30 cookies

Cream cheese makes a rich, tender dough with a wonderful flavor. These sweet cookies are flecked with bits of chopped pecan and topped with crisp whole pecans.

1½ cups flour
1 teaspoon baking powder
¼ teaspoon salt
½ cup (1 stick) unsalted butter, at room temperature
3 ounces cream cheese, at room temperature
¾ cup sugar
1 egg
1 teaspoon vanilla extract
1 cup finely chopped toasted pecans
30 whole pecans

1. Preheat the oven to 350°F; grease and flour 1 or 2 baking sheets. In a small bowl, stir or whisk together the flour, baking powder, and salt.

2. In a large bowl, cream the butter, cream cheese, and sugar. Add the egg and vanilla and beat again. Gradually add the flour mixture, blending well after each addition. Stir in the 1 cup chopped pecans.

3. Divide the dough into 3 equal pieces, preferably by weight. With moistened hands, divide and shape each piece of dough into 10 balls; you'll have a total of 30. Place the balls 1½ inches apart on the prepared

baking sheet. Press a whole pecan onto the top of each ball, flattening the ball slightly and making sure the pecan is firmly embedded in the dough.

4. Bake for 13 to 14 minutes, until the edges are nicely browned; the tops will remain pale tan. Transfer to wire racks to cool.

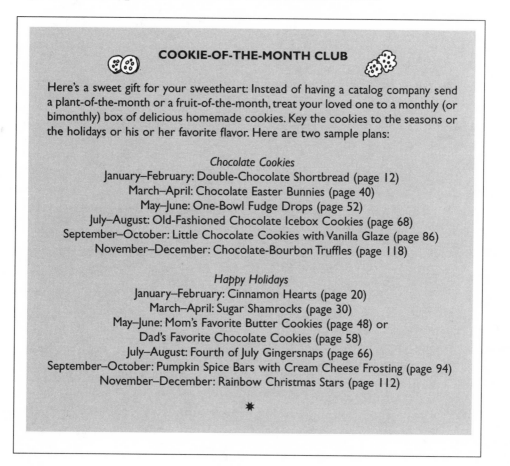

COOKIE-OF-THE-MONTH CLUB

Here's a sweet gift for your sweetheart: Instead of having a catalog company send a plant-of-the-month or a fruit-of-the-month, treat your loved one to a monthly (or bimonthly) box of delicious homemade cookies. Key the cookies to the seasons or the holidays or his or her favorite flavor. Here are two sample plans:

Chocolate Cookies
January–February: Double-Chocolate Shortbread (page 12)
March–April: Chocolate Easter Bunnies (page 40)
May–June: One-Bowl Fudge Drops (page 52)
July–August: Old-Fashioned Chocolate Icebox Cookies (page 68)
September–October: Little Chocolate Cookies with Vanilla Glaze (page 86)
November–December: Chocolate-Bourbon Truffles (page 118)

Happy Holidays
January–February: Cinnamon Hearts (page 20)
March–April: Sugar Shamrocks (page 30)
May–June: Mom's Favorite Butter Cookies (page 48) or
Dad's Favorite Chocolate Cookies (page 58)
July–August: Fourth of July Gingersnaps (page 66)
September–October: Pumpkin Spice Bars with Cream Cheese Frosting (page 94)
November–December: Rainbow Christmas Stars (page 112)

✳

February

WHEN THE WINTER BLUES *threaten to overwhelm you, lift your spirits with a baker's celebration: Cinnamon Hearts or Mocha-Glazed Vanilla Meringue Kisses for your valentine, Almond-Cherry Cups for Washington's birthday—and Ladyfingers just for fun.*

CINNAMON HEARTS

Makes about 3 1/2 dozen cookies

Crisp and crunchy, pretty as a picture. These are not your ordinary sugar cookies because they're made with brown sugar and topped with cinnamon sugar. A perfect gift for your sweetheart on Valentine's Day.

2 1/4 cups flour
3/4 teaspoon baking powder
1/4 teaspoon salt
1 teaspoon cinnamon
3/4 cup (1 1/2 sticks) unsalted butter, at room temperature
1/2 cup sugar
1/4 cup packed light brown sugar
1 egg
1/2 teaspoon vanilla extract
1 egg white stirred with 1 teaspoon water
Cinnamon sugar (1/3 cup sugar stirred with 1 teaspoon cinnamon)

1. In a medium-size bowl, stir or whisk together the flour, baking powder, salt, and cinnamon.

2. In a large bowl, cream the butter, sugar, and brown sugar. Add the egg and vanilla and beat well. Gradually add the flour mixture, blending well after each addition. Divide the dough in half, shape each piece into

an inch-thick disk, and wrap each disk in plastic. Refrigerate for 2 hours, or until firm enough to roll.

3. Preheat the oven to 350°F; grease 1 or 2 baking sheets. Dust a work surface and rolling pin with flour. Roll out 1 piece of dough to ⅛ inch thick. Cut with a 2½- to 3-inch heart-shaped cookie cutter. Use a spatula or pancake turner to place the cookies 1 inch apart on the prepared baking sheet. Gather up the excess dough for rerolling.

Repeat this process with the remaining piece of dough.

4. Brush the tops of 2 cookies with egg white mixture and sprinkle with cinnamon sugar. Repeat for all the remaining cookies.

5. Bake for 10 to 12 minutes, until the cookies are lightly browned; they will seem a bit soft, but they become crisp as they cool. Let the cookies cool on the baking sheet for 1 or 2 minutes, then transfer to wire racks to finish cooling.

MOCHA-GLAZED VANILLA MERINGUE KISSES

Makes about 10 dozen small cookies

This recipe makes a lot of kisses, but can you ever have too many? Note that these bite-size cookies are wheat-free.

3 egg whites, at room temperature
Pinch of salt
¼ teaspoon cream of tartar
¼ teaspoon fresh lemon juice
½ teaspoon vanilla extract
¾ cup superfine sugar

For the glaze:
4 ounces high-quality semisweet chocolate (such as
   Callebaut, Lindt, Valrhona or Ghirardelli), chopped
2 teaspoons vegetable oil
¼ cup water
1 tablespoon instant coffee granules, crushed to powder
Pinch of salt
½ teaspoon vanilla extract

1. Preheat the oven to 250°F; grease and flour 2 baking sheets. Have ready a 12-inch pastry bag fitted with a #2D (½-inch) star tip.

2. In a large bowl, beat the egg whites, salt, cream of tartar, lemon juice, and vanilla until the mixture holds soft peaks. Add the sugar

1 tablespoon at a time, beating until the whites are thick and smooth and stand in firm, glossy peaks, and the sugar is completely dissolved. Be sure to beat the mixture long enough.

3. Fill the pastry bag with half the meringue mixture. Pipe 1-inch-diameter kisses onto 1 prepared baking sheet, leaving ½ inch between kisses and using up all the meringue in the pastry bag.

Repeat this process with the remaining meringue mixture and the second baking sheet.

4. Bake both sheets at the same time (1 sheet on the middle shelf, 1 on the shelf above) for 40 minutes, reversing the positions of the baking sheets in the oven after 25 minutes. Turn off the heat and leave the kisses in the warm oven to dry out completely for 2 hours longer. Gently twist the kisses off the baking sheets or remove them with a small spatula if necessary. Brush excess flour off the bottoms.

5. Make the glaze: In a heavy saucepan over very low heat, melt the chocolate with the oil, water, and powdered coffee, stirring until the mixture is smooth and all the coffee has dissolved. Transfer the chocolate mixture to a small bowl and stir in the salt and vanilla.

6. Dip the top of each kiss into the glaze and let any excess drip off. (If necessary during the dipping process, reheat the glaze to maintain the proper consistency.) Place the kisses on waxed paper to let the glaze harden, about 2 hours.

ALMOND-CHERRY CUPS

Makes 2 dozen cups

These sweet tartlets are really special. Cream cheese dough lines the cups of tiny muffin pans, topped by a bit of cherry preserves and luscious almond filling. After baking, each cup is garnished with a whole cherry and a few almond slivers. Note that you'll need two gem muffin pans for this recipe.

For the cups:
½ cup (1 stick) unsalted butter, at room temperature
3 ounces cream cheese, at room temperature
1 cup flour stirred with a pinch of salt

For the filling and topping:
12-to 13-ounce jar of cherry preserves
¼ cup commercial pure almond paste (not marzipan)
½ cup sugar
2 egg yolks
3 tablespoons flour
3 tablespoons milk
Slivered toasted almonds

1. Make the cups: In a large bowl, cream the butter and cream cheese. Add the flour mixture and blend well. Divide the dough in half (preferably by weight), shape each piece into an inch-thick disk, and wrap each disk in plastic. Refrigerate for 1 hour, or until firm.

Preheat the oven to 400°F; have ready 2 gem muffin pans. Divide 1 package of dough into 12 equal pieces. With flour-dusted palms, roll each piece into a ball and place it in 1 cup of 1 gem pan. With flour-dusted fingers, press out the dough to line the bottom and sides of each cup evenly. (The cork from a wine bottle, dusted with flour, also works very well for this.) Use a fork to prick the dough on the bottom of each cup several times.

Repeat with the second package of dough and the second pan.

2. Remove 24 whole cherries from the jar of cherry preserves; set aside. Purée ½ cup preserves in a food processor; set aside. Wash the food processor bowl.

3. Make the almond filling: In the food processor, process the almond paste, sugar, egg yolks, flour, and milk until smooth.

4. Put ¾ teaspoon of the puréed cherry preserves in each prepared dough cup. Put a rounded teaspoon of the almond filling on top of the preserves in each cup.

5. Place the 2 gem pans on a baking sheet. Bake for 15 to 20 minutes, until both the filling and the dough are lightly browned. Allow the tartlets to cool in the gem pans, then remove carefully.

6. Add the topping: Crown each tartlet with 1 whole reserved cherry and a few slivered almonds.

LADYFINGERS

Makes about 3 dozen cookies

Homemade ladyfingers are made by piping an egg-based dough through a pastry bag. The cookies are tender but sturdy, delicate in flavor. Tip: Sandwich ladyfingers with jam, use them for making other desserts (such as tiramisù or trifle), or serve them with pudding, ice cream, or other creamy desserts.

4 eggs, separated into 2 large bowls	I cup flour stirred with ⅛ teaspoon
¼ cup superfine sugar	salt
½ cup confectioners' sugar	I teaspoon vanilla extract

1. Preheat the oven to 350°F; grease and flour 2 baking sheets. Have ready a pastry bag fitted with a ½-inch-diameter round tip; I use a plastic coupler with no tip at all.

2. Beat the egg yolks, the superfine sugar, and ¼ cup of the confectioners' sugar until thick and pale. Gradually sift and fold the flour into the yolk mixture; the dough will be very stiff.

3. With *clean, dry beaters*, beat the egg whites until foamy. Add the remaining ¼ cup confectioners' sugar and the vanilla and beat until the whites stand in firm, glossy, moist peaks. *Beat* a third of the egg white mixture into the stiff yolk mixture to lighten it; *fold* in the remaining egg white mixture.

4. Keeping your finger over the open tip, fill the pastry bag with about half the batter. Pipe 3 × 1-inch strips of batter, 1½ inches apart, onto the prepared baking sheets.

5. Bake for 9 to 11 minutes, until the cookies are dry and pale gold on top, with light brown edges; the undersides will be very light tan. Immediately transfer to wire racks to cool.

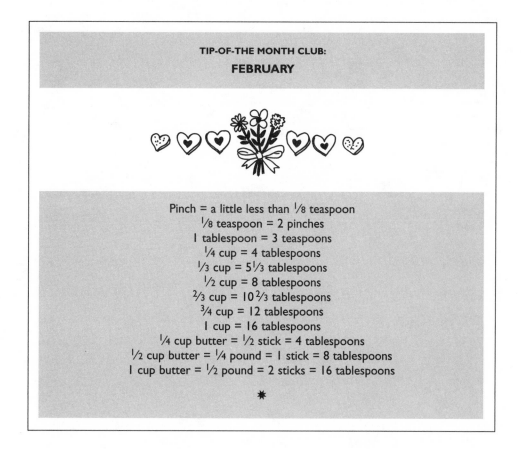

TIP-OF-THE MONTH CLUB:
FEBRUARY

Pinch = a little less than $1/8$ teaspoon
$1/8$ teaspoon = 2 pinches
1 tablespoon = 3 teaspoons
$1/4$ cup = 4 tablespoons
$1/3$ cup = $5 1/3$ tablespoons
$1/2$ cup = 8 tablespoons
$2/3$ cup = $10 2/3$ tablespoons
$3/4$ cup = 12 tablespoons
1 cup = 16 tablespoons
$1/4$ cup butter = $1/2$ stick = 4 tablespoons
$1/2$ cup butter = $1/4$ pound = 1 stick = 8 tablespoons
1 cup butter = $1/2$ pound = 2 sticks = 16 tablespoons

March

WIND AND RAIN *are a constant presence, and it seems as if spring will never come. It's time for a break: Invite a few friends over for an old-fashioned tea party—Currant Cookies, Lemon Teacakes with Lemon Glaze, and Cocoa Buttons make a wonderful trio of treats. Or try something interesting and fun to make—Hamantaschen with Two Fillings (the traditional cookies for the Jewish holiday called Purim), or Sugar Shamrocks for St. Patrick's Day.*

SUGAR SHAMROCKS

Makes about 3 1/2 dozen cookies

Classic sugar cookies, thin and crisp and sprinkled with green sugar, make a delicious St. Patrick's Day treat. You'll need a shamrock-shaped cookie cutter, about 3 inches wide. Tip: Use this recipe whenever you want perfect sugar cookies, cutting the dough with any cookie cutter you prefer.

2 cups plus 2 tablespoons flour
¾ teaspoon baking powder
¼ teaspoon salt
¾ cup (1½ sticks) unsalted butter, at room
   temperature
¾ cup sugar
1 egg
1 teaspoon vanilla extract
1 egg white stirred with 1 tablespoon water
Green sugar

1. In a small bowl, stir or whisk together the flour, baking powder, and salt.

2. In a large bowl, cream the butter and sugar. Add the egg and vanilla and beat again. Gradually add the flour mixture, blending well after each addition. Divide the dough in half, shape each piece into an inch-thick disk, and wrap each disk in plastic. Refrigerate for 1 hour, or until firm enough to roll.

3. Preheat the oven to 350°F; grease 1 or 2 baking sheets. Dust a work surface and rolling pin with flour. Roll out 1 piece of dough to ⅛ inch thick. Cut with a shamrock-shaped cookie cutter about 3 inches wide. Use a wide spatula or pancake turner to place the cookies 1 inch apart on the prepared baking sheet. Gather up the excess dough for rerolling.

Repeat this process with the second piece of dough.

4. Use a small pastry brush to spread a little egg white mixture on 1 cookie; immediately sprinkle with green sugar. Repeat with all the cookies.

5. Bake for 8 to 10 minutes, until the edges are lightly browned. Let the cookies cool on the baking sheet for about 1 minute, then carefully transfer to wire racks to finish cooling.

CURRANT COOKIES

Makes about 5 dozen cookies

An old-fashioned sort of cookie, crisp on the bottom and softer in the middle, studded with plenty of currants for extra sweetness. Perfect for snacking and afternoon tea.

1 cup (2 sticks) unsalted butter, at room temperature
1 cup sugar
2 eggs
1 teaspoon vanilla extract
3½ cups flour stirred with
  ¼ teaspoon salt

¼ cup sour cream stirred with
  ¼ teaspoon baking soda
¾ cup currants
Sugar for topping

1. Preheat the oven to 375°F; grease 1 or 2 baking sheets.

2. In a large bowl, cream the butter and sugar. Add the eggs and vanilla and beat until well blended. Add the flour mixture and the sour cream mixture alternately, in 3 parts, blending well after each addition. (You may want to blend the last portion of flour by hand.) Stir in the currants. Divide the dough in half.

3. Put 1 piece of dough on a flour-dusted work surface and knead 12 times. Dust the work surface and a rolling pin with more flour. Roll out the dough to a square about ⅛ inch thick. Sprinkle with sugar. With a sharp knife, cut the dough into 2-inch squares. Use a spatula or pancake turner to place the cookies 1 inch apart on the prepared baking sheet.

Gather up the excess dough for rerolling. Repeat this process with the second piece of dough.

4. Bake for 10 to 12 minutes, until the edges are browned; the tops will remain pale. Let the cookies cool on the baking sheet for about 1 minute, then transfer to wire racks to finish cooling.

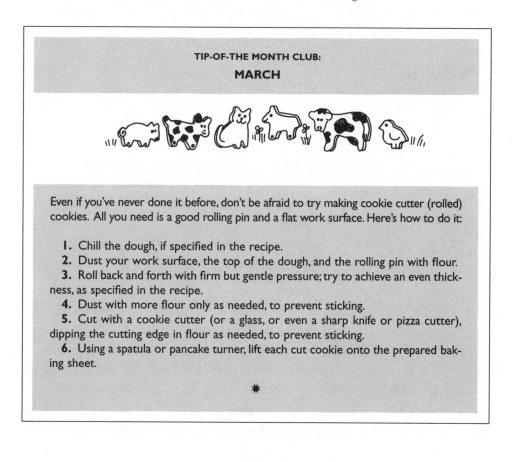

TIP-OF-THE MONTH CLUB:

MARCH

Even if you've never done it before, don't be afraid to try making cookie cutter (rolled) cookies. All you need is a good rolling pin and a flat work surface. Here's how to do it:

1. Chill the dough, if specified in the recipe.
2. Dust your work surface, the top of the dough, and the rolling pin with flour.
3. Roll back and forth with firm but gentle pressure; try to achieve an even thickness, as specified in the recipe.
4. Dust with more flour only as needed, to prevent sticking.
5. Cut with a cookie cutter (or a glass, or even a sharp knife or pizza cutter), dipping the cutting edge in flour as needed, to prevent sticking.
6. Using a spatula or pancake turner, lift each cut cookie onto the prepared baking sheet.

✳

LEMON TEACAKES WITH LEMON GLAZE

Makes about 3 1/2 dozen cookies

One of my favorites: tender, soft, lemony little cakes with crisp edges, topped with a rich lemon glaze. Tip: The glaze must be ready and waiting when the cookies come out of the oven, so make it first and set it aside until needed.

For the glaze:
1½ tablespoons unsalted butter, melted and cooled
½ teaspoon vanilla extract
1 teaspoon grated lemon rind
2 tablespoons fresh lemon juice
2 tablespoons milk
Pinch of salt
2 cups sifted confectioners' sugar

For the cookies:
1¾ cups flour
1 teaspoon baking powder
¼ teaspoon baking soda
¼ teaspoon salt
½ cup (1 stick) unsalted butter, at room temperature
¾ cup sugar
1 egg
1 teaspoon grated lemon rind
½ cup buttermilk

1. Make the glaze: In a large bowl, stir together the butter, vanilla, grated lemon rind, lemon juice, milk, and salt. Add the confectioners' sugar and beat until very smooth. Press a piece of plastic wrap directly onto the surface of the glaze, to prevent a crust from forming. Set aside until the cookies are baked.

2. Preheat the oven to 350°F; grease 1 or 2 baking sheets. In a small bowl, stir or whisk together the flour, baking powder, baking soda, and salt.

3. In a large bowl, cream the butter and sugar. Add the egg and grated lemon rind and beat well. Add the flour mixture and buttermilk alternately, in 3 parts, blending well after each addition.

4. Drop the dough by scant tablespoons, 1½ inches apart, onto the prepared baking sheet.

5. Bake for 12 to 14 minutes, until pale tan with light brown edges. Immediately transfer the cookies to wire racks and allow them to cool for a couple of minutes. While the cookies are still very warm, spread about ½ teaspoon of the glaze on each one. Let the cookies finish cooling on the racks; the glaze will set as the cookies cool.

SANDWICH COOKIES ON THE FLY

If you love sandwich cookies, try making your own with homemade cookies and your choice of fillings. Thin, crisp icebox cookies (such as Old-Fashioned Chocolate Icebox Cookies, page 68, or Butterscotch Icebox Cookies, page 96) make wonderful sandwiches, put together with cream cheese frosting (page 94) or thick vanilla glaze (page 86). Crisp Orange Cookies (page 106) work well, too, with those fillings. For a bigger, softer sandwich, Big Sugar Cookies (page 84) or Dad's Favorite Chocolate Cookies (page 58) are delicious when filled with frosting or glaze. Other filling possibilities: peanut or almond butter; jam or preserves; marmalade; fruit butter; sweetened cream cheese.

✴

COCOA BUTTONS

Makes about 5 dozen cookies

Without the final sprinkling of confectioners' sugar, these small, crisp, melt-in-your-mouth cookies are more chocolaty than sweet—which many people prefer. I like the added sweetness, but you may take your pick.

2 cups flour
⅓ cup cocoa powder, sifted
⅛ teaspoon salt
1 cup (2 sticks) unsalted butter, at room temperature

1 cup confectioners' sugar, sifted
1 egg yolk
¼ cup milk
Extra confectioners' sugar for dusting

1. Preheat the oven to 350°F; have ready 1 or 2 ungreased baking sheets. In a small bowl, stir or whisk together the flour, cocoa, and salt.

2. In a large bowl, cream the butter until light. Add the confectioners' sugar and beat again. Add the egg yolk and milk and beat for 4 minutes. Gradually add the flour mixture, blending well after each addition.

3. Drop the dough by neatly rounded teaspoons, 1½ inches apart, on the ungreased baking sheet.

4. Bake for 10 minutes. Let the cookies cool on the baking sheet for 1 or 2 minutes, then transfer to wire racks. Using a fine sieve, generously dust the tops of the hot cookies with confectioners' sugar. Allow the cookies to cool completely on the wire racks.

HAMANTASCHEN WITH TWO FILLINGS

Makes about 4 dozen cookies

Hamantaschen resemble three-cornered hats, and indeed they are named for the hat worn by Prince Haman in the biblical story of Queen Esther; the diagram on page 38 will show you what these cookies should look like. Take your choice of prune or walnut filling; each recipe below makes enough to fill all the cookies.

For the prune filling:
1 cup pitted prunes
½ cup water
2 tablespoons sugar
½ teaspoon grated orange rind
¼ teaspoon almond extract

For the nut filling:
1½ cups finely chopped walnuts
1 teaspoon cinnamon
½ cup puréed apricot jam

For the dough:
3¼ cups flour
½ teaspoon baking powder
½ teaspoon salt
6 tablespoons unsalted butter,
   at room temperature
2 eggs plus 2 egg yolks
⅔ cup honey

1. Make the prune *or* the nut filling: For the prune filling, put the prunes, water, and sugar in a heavy saucepan and simmer, partially covered, until the prunes are soft and the water is almost gone, 8 to 10 minutes. Put the prune mixture in a food processor with the grated orange rind and almond extract and process until smooth. Set aside to cool.

For the nut filling, put all the ingredients in a medium-size bowl and stir well. Set aside until needed.

2. Preheat the oven to 350°F; have ready 2 ungreased baking sheets. In a medium-size bowl, stir or whisk together 3 cups of the flour, the baking powder, and the salt.

3. In a large bowl, cream the butter. Add the eggs, egg yolks, and honey and beat well. Gradually add the flour mixture, blending well after each addition. Add the remaining ¼ cup flour and stir in by hand; the dough will be stiff.

4. Divide the dough in half; there's no need to chill it. Dust a work surface and rolling pin with flour. Roll out 1 piece of dough to a little more than ⅛ inch thick and cut with a round cookie cutter 3 inches in diameter. Use a large spatula or pancake turner to place the cookies ¼ inch apart on one of the ungreased baking sheets. Gather up the excess dough for rerolling.

Repeat this process with the second piece of dough.

5. Place a rounded teaspoon of filling in the center of each cookie; flatten the filling slightly with the back of a spoon. Using a small pastry brush, moisten the entire edge of 1 cookie with water; fold the edges up to make a 3-cornered "hat" and pinch together firmly at the corners, as shown.

Repeat this process with all the remaining cookies.

6. Bake for 14 to 15 minutes, until the edges are lightly browned and the bottoms are brown. Immediately transfer the cookies to wire racks to cool.

April

THERE'S A SCENT of freshness and hope in the air. Spring is really on the way, and the crocuses and daffodils are pushing spiky green leaves up through the damp ground. It's the season for Chocolate Easter Bunnies and, for Passover, Coconut Macaroons. Between holidays, bake up a batch of Pistachio Biscotti or a pan of Glazed Banana-Nut Squares.

CHOCOLATE EASTER BUNNIES

Makes about 3 1/2 dozen cookies

These thin, crisp chocolate bunnies will disappear as fast as the carrots in a Bugs Bunny cartoon. You'll need a rabbit-shaped cookie cutter and a tube of ready-made white icing (with your own tips) for decorating the bunnies.

2¼ cups flour
¾ teaspoon baking powder
¼ teaspoon salt
¾ cup (1½ sticks) unsalted butter, at room
  temperature
¾ cup sugar
1 egg plus 1 egg yolk
1 teaspoon vanilla extract

1. Preheat the oven to 350°F; grease 1 or 2 baking sheets. In a small bowl, stir or whisk together the flour, baking powder, and salt.
2. In a large bowl, cream the butter and sugar. Add the egg, egg yolk,

and vanilla and beat until well blended. Add the melted chocolate and blend again. Gradually add the flour mixture, blending well after each addition.

3. Divide the dough into 3 pieces; there's no need to chill it. Dust a work surface with flour. With flour-dusted hands, pat out 1 piece of dough to about $\frac{1}{4}$ inch thick. Important: The dough will be a bit crumbly, so keep patting the edges together. Now dust a rolling pin with flour and carefully roll the dough to about $\frac{1}{8}$ inch thick. Cut with a bunny-shaped cookie cutter. Use a large spatula or pancake turner to place the cookies 1 inch apart on the prepared baking sheet. Gather up the excess dough for rerolling; reroll only once, because after that the dough will have absorbed so much flour that the cookies would be tough when baked.

Repeat this process with the remaining pieces of dough.

4. Bake for 10 to 11 minutes, until the cookies are dry on top and feel firm to the touch. Let the cookies cool on the baking sheet for 1 minute, then transfer carefully to wire racks to finish cooling. A cooled cookie will be crisp.

PISTACHIO BISCOTTI

Makes about 32 cookies

Crisp, crunchy biscotti are much easier to make than you probably imagine. This version, with pistachios scattered all through, makes a perfect light dessert, accompanied by ripe fruit and a sweet wine (or good coffee) for dipping. Note that there are no dairy products in this cookie.

4 eggs
2 teaspoons vanilla extract
2½ cups flour
1 teaspoon baking powder
¼ teaspoon baking soda
¼ teaspoon salt
½ cup sugar
½ cup packed light brown sugar
1½ cups whole, shelled, unsalted pistachios

1. Preheat the oven to 325°F; grease 1 baking sheet. For step 5, have ready 2 ungreased baking sheets. In a medium-size bowl, whisk or beat together the eggs and vanilla.

2. In a large bowl, stir or whisk together 2 cups of the flour and the baking powder, baking soda, salt, sugar, and brown sugar. Add the egg mixture and stir by hand until most of the flour is moistened. Add the pistachios and mix again; the dough will be stiff and sticky. Add the remaining ½ cup of flour and work it in.

3. Divide the dough into 2 equal parts and place on the greased baking sheet. With flour-dusted hands, shape each piece into a loaf about 9 inches long, 3½ inches wide, and ¾ inch high. Leave about 4 inches between the loaves on the baking sheet.

4. Bake for 30 minutes. Reduce the oven temperature to 300°F. Use a serrated knife to score the top of each loaf with shallow cuts ½ inch apart, straight across. Let the loaves cool on the baking sheet for 10 minutes.

5. On a cutting board, use the serrated knife to cut through each loaf on the scored lines, making ½-inch-wide slices. Place the slices flat on the ungreased baking sheets, ½ inch apart, and bake for 15 minutes at the reduced heat. Turn the slices over and bake for another 15 minutes. Finally, turn the oven off and leave the biscotti in the warm oven to dry out for a final 15 minutes. Transfer to wire racks and allow to cool completely.

TIP-OF-THE-MONTH CLUB:
APRIL

Time for spring cleaning and organizing? Start in the kitchen. If you bake frequently, it makes sense to stash all your baking supplies in one general area: Keep all your baking ingredients (such as baking powder, confectioners' sugar, nuts, and chocolate chips) on one shelf; store all your baking equipment (such as pans, rolling pin, and wire racks) in a nearby cabinet.

✳

COCONUT MACAROONS

Makes about 4 1/2 dozen cookies

These beautiful tan macaroons with lightly browned edges have crisp tops that look a bit like meringues—but inside they are as chewy and rich as a maca-roon should be.

3 egg whites
1 cup sugar
2½ tablespoons flour stirred with ⅛ teaspoon salt
1 teaspoon vanilla extract
½ teaspoon almond extract
2 cups sweetened shredded coconut

1. Preheat the oven to 325°F; grease and flour 2 baking sheets.
2. In a large bowl, beat the egg whites until they form soft peaks. Add the sugar 1 tablespoon at a time, beating well after each addition; the mixture will be thick and glossy. Add the flour, vanilla, and almond extract and beat again. Fold in the coconut.
3. Drop the batter by rounded teaspoons, 1½ inches apart, onto the prepared baking sheets.
4. Bake for 12 to 14 minutes, until tan and crisp on top and lightly browned on the bottom. Transfer to wire racks to cool.

GLAZED BANANA-NUT SQUARES

Makes 24 squares

If you like a mild banana flavor, you'll love these bar cookies. They have a terrific texture, and the super-simple glaze and chopped-walnut topping add a wonderful richness.

For the glaze:
¼ cup heavy cream
1 cup confectioners' sugar, sifted
1 teaspoon vanilla extract
Pinch of salt

For the cookies:
1½ cups flour
1 teaspoon baking powder
½ teaspoon salt
½ cup (1 stick) salted margarine,
    at room temperature
½ cup sugar
½ cup packed light brown sugar
1 egg
1 cup mashed ripe bananas (about
    2 medium bananas)
1 cup chopped walnuts

1. Make the glaze: In a medium-size bowl, beat the cream and confectioners' sugar until smooth. Beat in the vanilla and salt. Cover with plastic wrap pressed directly onto the glaze, to prevent a crust from forming. Set aside.

2. Preheat the oven to 350°F; grease a 9 × 13-inch baking pan. In a small bowl, stir or whisk together the flour, baking powder, and salt.

3. In a large bowl, cream the margarine, sugar, and brown sugar. Add the egg and beat well. Add the flour mixture and the bananas alternately, in 3 parts, blending well after each addition. Stir in ½ cup of the walnuts.

4. Spread the batter evenly in the prepared pan.

5. Bake for 25 minutes, until the top is golden, the edges are brown and pulling away from the sides of the pan, and a toothpick inserted in the center of the pan comes out clean. Let the pan cool on a wire rack for about 15 minutes, until just warm.

6. Spread the glaze evenly over the top and immediately sprinkle with the remaining ½ cup walnuts. Let cool completely. Run a sharp knife around the edge of the pan, then cut into 24 squares (4 squares by 6 squares).

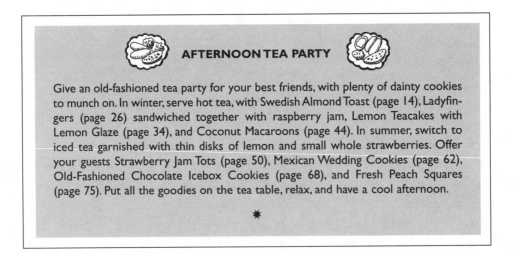

AFTERNOON TEA PARTY

Give an old-fashioned tea party for your best friends, with plenty of dainty cookies to munch on. In winter, serve hot tea, with Swedish Almond Toast (page 14), Ladyfingers (page 26) sandwiched together with raspberry jam, Lemon Teacakes with Lemon Glaze (page 34), and Coconut Macaroons (page 44). In summer, switch to iced tea garnished with thin disks of lemon and small whole strawberries. Offer your guests Strawberry Jam Tots (page 50), Mexican Wedding Cookies (page 62), Old-Fashioned Chocolate Icebox Cookies (page 68), and Fresh Peach Squares (page 75). Put all the goodies on the tea table, relax, and have a cool afternoon.

✳

May

IN ADDITION TO *being a glorious time of sunshine and mild weather, May is also Mom's month. Impress her on her special day with Mom's Favorite Butter Cookies and Linzer Hearts. May is strawberry season, too, which is fun to celebrate with Strawberry Jam Tots. Any season is chocolate season, so surprise your family with a batch of easy-as-pie One-Bowl Fudge Drops.*

MOM'S FAVORITE BUTTER COOKIES

Makes 4 dozen cookies

In my family these are also called Ethel's cookies, though no one knows who Ethel was. The neat squares are thin and dense, but also tender and buttery. They have a light orange flavor, the delicious sweetness of brown sugar, and a pretty almond topping.

2½ cups flour
¼ teaspoon baking powder
¼ teaspoon salt
1 cup (2 sticks) unsalted butter, at room temperature
1 cup packed light brown sugar
1 egg, separated
2 teaspoons grated orange rind
½ cup chopped almonds (with or without skins)

1. Preheat the oven to 375°F; grease a 10½ × 15½-inch jelly roll pan. In a medium-size bowl, stir or whisk together the flour, baking powder, and salt.

2. In a large bowl, cream the butter and brown sugar. Add the egg yolk and grated rind and beat well. Gradually add the flour mixture, blending well after each addition.

3. With moistened fingers, pat out the dough evenly in the prepared pan. Brush with the egg white and sprinkle evenly with the chopped

almonds; use a spatula or pancake turner to press the almonds lightly into the dough.

4. Bake for 12 to 14 minutes, until the edges are browned and the top looks dry. Let the pan cool on a wire rack, then use a sharp knife to cut into 48 squares (6 squares by 8 squares).

STRAWBERRY JAM TOTS

Makes about 4 1/2 dozen cookies

Jam tots are small, buttery cookies with jam-filled centers. You need not use straw-berry jam, of course; feel free to use any favorite flavor. Note that you'll need a thimble or a small cork for making the depressions in the centers of the cookies.

3/4 cup (1 1/2 sticks) unsalted butter,
  at room temperature
1/2 cup sugar
1 egg plus 1 egg yolk

1 teaspoon vanilla extract
1 1/2 cups flour stirred with
  1/2 teaspoon salt
Strawberry jam

1. In a large bowl, cream the butter and sugar. Add the egg, egg yolk, and vanilla and beat again. Gradually add the flour mixture, blending well after each addition. The dough will be sticky. Divide the dough in half, shape each piece into an inch-thick disk, and wrap each disk in plastic. Refrigerate for 2 hours, or until firm enough to shape.

2. Preheat the oven to 375°F; grease 1 or 2 baking sheets. Work with 1 disk of dough at a time. With flour-dusted hands, shape the dough into 1-inch-diameter balls. Place the balls 1 1/2 inches apart on the prepared baking sheet.

Repeat this process with the second piece of dough.

3. Bake for 5 minutes. Remove from the oven and carefully use a thimble or a small cork to make a deep depression in the center of each cookie. Return the baking sheet to the oven and bake for 8 to 9 minutes longer, until the edges are lightly browned. Immediately transfer to wire racks to cool.

4. Fill the depressions with strawberry jam, or any other favorite jam.

COOKIE DECORATIONS ON THE FLY

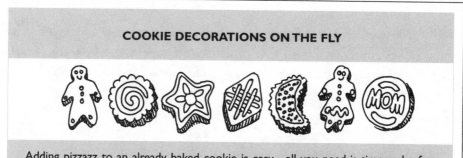

Adding pizzazz to an already baked cookie is easy—all you need is time and a few simple ingredients. Dad's Favorite Chocolate Cookies (page 58), Old-Fashioned Chocolate Icebox Cookies (page 68), Big Sugar Cookies (page 84), Crisp Orange Cookies (page 106), Gingerbread Cookie Ornaments (page 114), and any shape of cookie made with the Sugar Shamrocks dough (page 30) are all good candidates for decorations.

•Spread one cookie at a time with any of the light-colored glazes, icing, or frosting in the book (such as vanilla glaze, page 86; lemon glaze, page 34; vanilla icing, page 10; cream cheese frosting, page 94). While the glaze is still soft and sticky, press decorations into it. Try whole or chopped nuts, miniature chocolate chips, currants or raisins, bits of dried fruit, small candies, multicolored or chocolate sprinkles, multi-colored dots, or colored sugar.

•Pipe simple designs on the cookies, with ready-to-use tubes of decorating icing and your own round or star-shaped decorating tips. Spirals, squiggles, dots, grids, silly faces, names, and messages are all fun to do.

•Drizzle chocolate glaze (page 116) over light-colored cookies.

•Sift confectioners' sugar over dark-colored cookies.

✳

ONE-BOWL FUDGE DROPS

Makes about 7 dozen small cookies

Small crisp cookies—a bite or two each—with a fudgy chocolate flavor enhanced by chocolate chips. Quick and easy to make when you want a chocolate fix. Note that only one bowl (and no mixer) is needed.

5 ounces unsweetened chocolate, chopped
½ cup (1 stick) unsalted butter
2 tablespoons light corn syrup
1 cup plus 2 tablespoons sugar
1 teaspoon vanilla extract

¼ cup milk
3 eggs
1½ cups flour stirred with ½ teaspoon salt
⅔ cup semisweet chocolate chips

1. Preheat the oven to 350°F; grease and flour 1 or 2 baking sheets.

2. In a large metal bowl set over a saucepan containing 2 inches of barely simmering water, melt the unsweetened chocolate, the butter, and the corn syrup, *whisking* until smooth. Remove the bowl from the saucepan and allow to cool until warm. Whisk in the sugar, vanilla, and milk, then whisk in the eggs one at a time. Add the flour mixture and *stir* just until mixed. Stir in the chocolate chips.

3. Drop the dough by rounded teaspoons, 1 inch apart, onto the prepared baking sheet.

4. Bake for 9 to 10 minutes, until the cookies look dry on top but are still soft to the touch. Immediately transfer to wire racks to cool.

LINZER HEARTS

Makes about 2 1/2 dozen sandwich cookies

Each linzer heart is a pair of crisp sugar cookies (one with a heart-shaped cutout) filled with raspberry jam. To make the cookies you'll need two heart-shaped cookie cutters—one about 3 inches wide for the cookies, and another that's 1 inch wide for cutting out the centers.

2¾ cups flour
1½ teaspoons baking powder
½ teaspoon salt
½ teaspoon nutmeg
½ cup (1 stick) unsalted butter, at room temperature
1 cup sugar
1 egg
⅓ cup milk
1½ teaspoons vanilla extract
Seedless raspberry jam
Confectioners' sugar for sifting

1. In a medium-size bowl, stir or whisk together 2½ cups of the flour and the baking powder, salt, and nutmeg.

2. In a large bowl, cream the butter and sugar. Add the egg, milk, and vanilla and beat well. Gradually add the flour mixture, blending well after each addition. Mix in the remaining ¼ cup flour by hand. Divide the dough in half (preferably by weight), shape each piece into an inch-thick disk, and wrap each disk in plastic. Refrigerate for 2 hours, or until firm enough to roll.

3. Preheat the oven to 375°F; grease 2 baking sheets. Dust a work surface and rolling pin with flour. Roll out 1 piece of dough to ⅛ inch thick. Use a 3-inch-wide heart-shaped cookie cutter to cut an even number of cookies. With a spatula or pancake turner, place half the cookies 1 inch apart on *each* prepared baking sheet. Gather up the excess dough, reroll, and repeat this process. Using a 1-inch-wide heart-shaped cookie cutter, cut and remove a heart from the center of all the cookies on 1 of the baking sheets. Discard the removed hearts and all leftover dough.

4. Bake the whole hearts for 9 to 10 minutes, until the edges are lightly browned; bake the cutout hearts for 8 to 9 minutes, watching carefully to prevent overbaking. Immediately transfer to wire racks to cool.

5. With the oven still at 375°, repeat steps 3 and 4 using the second piece of dough.

6. Spread about ½ teaspoon of raspberry jam on each whole heart cookie; top with a cutout heart cookie to make a sandwich. Using a fine strainer, sift a little confectioners' sugar over each sandwich.

June

A MONTH OF *happy occasions—Father's Day, graduations, weddings, and honeymoons—and there's a cookie for every one. Bake Dad's Favorite Chocolate Cookies for your favorite father, Mexican-Wedding Cookies for the happy couple, and Aloha Cookies for a sweet send-off. Then treat yourself to the first outing of the summer, with Melt-in-Your-Mouth Cornmeal Cookies tucked into the picnic basket.*

DAD'S FAVORITE CHOCOLATE COOKIES

Makes about 18 big cookies

These cookies are thin and crisp and big. The preparation is easy: Simply shape the dough into balls and flatten with the bottom of a glass. Wonderful for a June picnic, packed in a sturdy plastic container to prevent breakage.

1¾ cups flour
¾ teaspoon baking powder
½ teaspoon salt
½ cup (1 stick) unsalted butter, at room temperature
¾ cup sugar
1 egg
2 ounces semisweet chocolate, melted and cooled
1 teaspoon vanilla extract

1. Preheat the oven to 375°F; grease 2 or 3 baking sheets. In a small bowl, stir or whisk together the flour, baking powder, and salt.

2. In a large bowl, cream the butter and sugar. Add the egg, melted chocolate, and vanilla and beat until well blended. Gradually add the flour mixture, beating well after each addition.

3. Shape the dough into 1½-inch-diameter balls. Place the balls about 3 inches apart on one of the prepared baking sheets. Use the flat bottom of a glass, dipped in sugar, to flatten each ball to about ⅛ inch thick; each cookie will be 3½ to 4 inches in diameter. Because the cookies are so large, you'll only be able to fit about 6 on each baking sheet.

4. Bake for 9 to 10 minutes, until the edges are slightly browned and the tops are dry and crisp-looking. Let the cookies cool almost completely on the baking sheet, then transfer to wire racks to finish cooling.

COOKIE WRAP-UPS

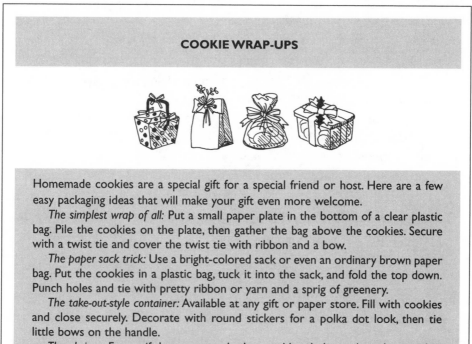

Homemade cookies are a special gift for a special friend or host. Here are a few easy packaging ideas that will make your gift even more welcome.

The simplest wrap of all: Put a small paper plate in the bottom of a clear plastic bag. Pile the cookies on the plate, then gather the bag above the cookies. Secure with a twist tie and cover the twist tie with ribbon and a bow.

The paper sack trick: Use a bright-colored sack or even an ordinary brown paper bag. Put the cookies in a plastic bag, tuck it into the sack, and fold the top down. Punch holes and tie with pretty ribbon or yarn and a sprig of greenery.

The take-out-style container: Available at any gift or paper store. Fill with cookies and close securely. Decorate with round stickers for a polka dot look, then tie little bows on the handle.

The obvious: Fancy gift boxes, pretty baskets and bowls, large clear glass or plastic jars, plastic kitchen containers, and old-fashioned cookie tins protect the cookies and can be reused—a double present.

MELT-IN-YOUR-MOUTH CORNMEAL COOKIES

Makes about 3 1/2 dozen cookies

Here's an icebox cookie that's extremely easy to make and a bit out of the ordinary. It's made with flour and cornmeal, which gives it an extra crunch. These thin, crisp cookies spread to about 3 inches in diameter—a nice big handful of cookie.

1 1/4 cups flour	1 cup packed light brown sugar
1 cup yellow cornmeal	2 egg yolks
1/4 teaspoon salt	1 teaspoon vanilla extract
1 cup (2 sticks) unsalted butter, at room temperature	

1. In a small bowl, stir or whisk together the flour, cornmeal, and salt.

2. In a large bowl, cream the butter and brown sugar. Add the egg yolks and vanilla and beat well. Gradually add the flour mixture, blending well after each addition.

3. Divide the dough in half and place each half on a piece of plastic wrap. Using the plastic to help, shape each half into a smooth log about 2 inches in diameter. Wrap snugly in the plastic and refrigerate for several hours, until firm, turning and smoothing the logs occasionally to maintain the cylindrical shape.

4. Preheat the oven to 400°F; grease 1 or 2 baking sheets. Unwrap 1 log of dough and use a sharp knife to cut it into ³/₈-inch-thick slices. Place the slices 1 1/2 to 2 inches apart on the prepared baking sheet; the cookies spread quite a bit, so don't stint on the spacing.

Repeat with the second log or reserve it for future use.

5. Bake for 8 to 9 minutes, until the edges are browned and the tops are golden. Don't overbake. Let the cookies cool for 1 or 2 minutes on the baking sheet, then transfer carefully to wire racks to finish cooling. The cookies are soft and fragile when hot, but they cool into crisp wafers.

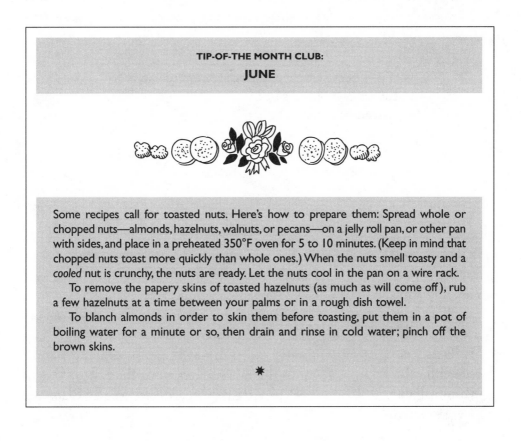

TIP-OF-THE MONTH CLUB:

JUNE

Some recipes call for toasted nuts. Here's how to prepare them: Spread whole or chopped nuts—almonds, hazelnuts, walnuts, or pecans—on a jelly roll pan, or other pan with sides, and place in a preheated 350°F oven for 5 to 10 minutes. (Keep in mind that chopped nuts toast more quickly than whole ones.) When the nuts smell toasty and a *cooled* nut is crunchy, the nuts are ready. Let the nuts cool in the pan on a wire rack.

To remove the papery skins of toasted hazelnuts (as much as will come off), rub a few hazelnuts at a time between your palms or in a rough dish towel.

To blanch almonds in order to skin them before toasting, put them in a pot of boiling water for a minute or so, then drain and rinse in cold water; pinch off the brown skins.

✳

MEXICAN WEDDING COOKIES

Makes about 4 1/2 dozen cookies

Sophisticated and mouthwatering, these buttery, bite-size nuggets—packed with hazelnuts, adrift in a cloud of confectioners' sugar—are worthy of any wedding celebration. Tip: *Don't make them any bigger than the recipe specifies; they're meant to be small.*

½ cup (1 stick) unsalted butter, at room temperature
⅓ cup confectioners' sugar
1½ teaspoons vanilla extract
1 cup flour stirred with ¼ teaspoon salt
1 cup toasted finely chopped hazelnuts (with skins)
Sifted confectioners' sugar for rolling

1. Preheat the oven to 350°F; have ready 1 or 2 ungreased baking sheets.

2. In a large bowl, cream the butter and the ⅓ cup confectioners' sugar. Beat in the vanilla. Gradually add the flour mixture, blending well after each addition. Stir in the chopped hazelnuts.

3. With moistened hands, shape the dough into 1-inch-diameter balls. Place the balls 1 inch apart on the ungreased baking sheet.

4. Bake for 13 to 14 minutes, until dry-looking on top and lightly browned on the bottom. Remove the hot cookies from the baking sheets and immediately roll in a bowl of sifted confectioners' sugar. Place on wire racks to cool.

ALOHA COOKIES

Makes about 3 dozen cookies

Plump mounds chock-full of chopped pineapple, sweet coconut, and luscious macadamia nuts. Serve with iced tea or lemonade for a summer treat.

1¾ cups flour
1½ teaspoons baking powder
¼ teaspoon salt
10 tablespoons (1 stick plus 2 tablespoons) unsalted butter, at room temperature

¾ cup sugar
2 eggs
1 teaspoon vanilla extract
½ cup chopped dried pineapple
¾ cup sweetened shredded coconut

1. Preheat the oven to 375°F; grease 1 or 2 baking sheets. In a small bowl, stir or whisk together the flour, baking powder, and salt.

2. In a large bowl, cream the butter and sugar. Add the eggs and vanilla and beat well. Gradually add the flour mixture, blending well after each addition. Stir in the pineapple, coconut, and macadamia nuts.

3. Drop the dough by tablespoons, 1½ inches apart, on the prepared baking sheet.

4. Bake for 10 to 12 minutes, until the edges are browned and the tops are firm to the touch. Let the cookies cool for 1 or 2 minutes on the baking sheet, then transfer to wire racks to finish cooling.

July

THINK FIRECRACKERS and Fourth of July Gingersnaps; trips to the shore and Beach Party Pecan Sandies; tall, cool drinks and Old-Fashioned Chocolate Icebox Cookies. Think juicy summer fruit, too, and try a pan of Blueberry—Cream Cheese Squares.

FOURTH OF JULY GINGERSNAPS

Makes about 5 1/2 dozen cookies

Wake up summer appetites with these spicy, easy-to-make cookies, one of the best gingersnaps you'll ever taste. Try serving them with a chilled fruit salad of melon, peaches, and berries.

2 cups flour
1 teaspoon baking soda
1/2 teaspoon salt
1 teaspoon ground ginger
1/2 teaspoon cinnamon
1/2 cup (1 stick) unsalted butter,
   at room temperature

1/2 cup sugar
1/2 cup packed light brown sugar
1 egg
1/4 cup unsulphured molasses
   (not blackstrap)
Sugar for topping

1. Preheat the oven to 325°F; grease 1 or 2 baking sheets. In a medium-size bowl, stir or whisk together the flour, baking soda, salt, and spices.

2. In a large bowl, cream the butter, sugar, and brown sugar. Add the egg and molasses and beat well. Gradually add the flour mixture, blending well after each addition.

3. With flour-dusted hands, shape the dough into 1-inch-diameter balls. Place the balls 2 inches apart on the prepared baking sheet. With a fork dipped in sugar, flatten each drop to about 1/4 inch thick; sprinkle with a little more sugar.

4. Bake for 12 to 13 minutes, until the tops are dry and the edges

look crisp. Let the cookies cool on the baking sheet for 1 or 2 minutes, then transfer to wire racks to finish cooling.

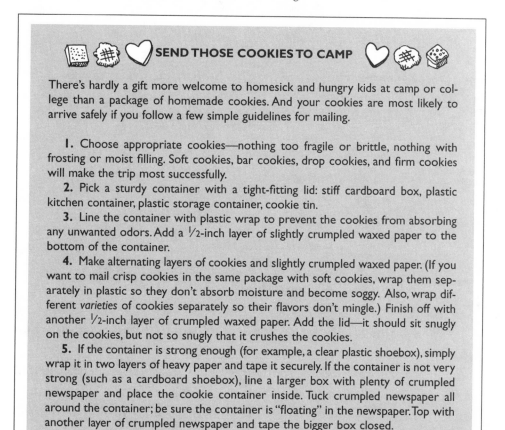

SEND THOSE COOKIES TO CAMP

There's hardly a gift more welcome to homesick and hungry kids at camp or college than a package of homemade cookies. And your cookies are most likely to arrive safely if you follow a few simple guidelines for mailing.

1. Choose appropriate cookies—nothing too fragile or brittle, nothing with frosting or moist filling. Soft cookies, bar cookies, drop cookies, and firm cookies will make the trip most successfully.

2. Pick a sturdy container with a tight-fitting lid: stiff cardboard box, plastic kitchen container, plastic storage container, cookie tin.

3. Line the container with plastic wrap to prevent the cookies from absorbing any unwanted odors. Add a ½-inch layer of slightly crumpled waxed paper to the bottom of the container.

4. Make alternating layers of cookies and slightly crumpled waxed paper. (If you want to mail crisp cookies in the same package with soft cookies, wrap them separately in plastic so they don't absorb moisture and become soggy. Also, wrap different *varieties* of cookies separately so their flavors don't mingle.) Finish off with another ½-inch layer of crumpled waxed paper. Add the lid—it should sit snugly on the cookies, but not so snugly that it crushes the cookies.

5. If the container is strong enough (for example, a clear plastic shoebox), simply wrap it in two layers of heavy paper and tape it securely. If the container is not very strong (such as a cardboard shoebox), line a larger box with plenty of crumpled newspaper and place the cookie container inside. Tuck crumpled newspaper all around the container; be sure the container is "floating" in the newspaper. Top with another layer of crumpled newspaper and tape the bigger box closed.

OLD-FASHIONED CHOCOLATE
ICEBOX COOKIES

Makes about 4 1/2 dozen cookies

Sometimes simple is better—and these tasty chocolate wafers are simply the best. Delicious for snacks and picnics and perfect for dessert when served with ice cream, pudding, or fruit. So good you could eat a dozen.

2¼ cups flour
1 teaspoon baking powder
½ teaspoon salt
½ cup (1 stick) unsalted butter, at room temperature
1 cup sugar
2 eggs
2 ounces unsweetened chocolate, melted and cooled
1 teaspoon vanilla extract

1. In a medium-size bowl, stir or whisk together the flour, baking powder, and salt.

2. In a large bowl, cream the butter and sugar. Add the eggs, melted chocolate, and vanilla and beat well. Gradually add the flour mixture, blending well after each addition. The dough will be soft.

3. Divide the dough in half and place each half on a piece of plastic wrap. Using the plastic to help, shape each half into a smooth log about 2 inches in diameter. Wrap snugly in the plastic and refrigerate for sev-

eral hours, until firm, turning and smoothing the logs occasionally to maintain the cylindrical shape.

4. Preheat the oven to 400°F; grease 1 or 2 baking sheets. Unwrap 1 log of dough and use a sharp knife to cut it into ⅛-inch-thick slices. Place the slices 1 inch apart on the prepared baking sheet.

Repeat with the second log or reserve it for future use.

5. Bake for 8 to 9 minutes; a cooled cookie will be firm and crisp. Be very careful not to burn the edges. Let the cookies cool for 1 minute on the baking sheet, then transfer to wire racks to finish cooling.

TIP-OF-THE-MONTH CLUB:
JULY

Cool off with homemade ice cream sandwiches: Soften and spread your favorite flavor of ice cream between two homemade cookies; wrap in plastic or foil and freeze until firm. Old-Fashioned Chocolate Icebox Cookies (page 68), Butterscotch Icebox Cookies (page 96), and Big Sugar Cookies (page 84) are all good choices for making these treats.

❋

BLUEBERRY–CREAM CHEESE SQUARES

Makes 25 squares

Sensational little squares with a crisp cookie bottom and a rich cream cheese custard topped with a generous layer of fresh blueberries. Best eaten on the day they're made.

For the bottom layer:
½ cup (1 stick) unsalted butter, at room temperature
⅓ cup sugar
1 teaspoon grated lemon rind
1⅓ cups flour stirred with
⅛ teaspoon salt

For the topping:
3 ounces cream cheese, at room temperature
⅔ cup sugar
2 eggs
1 teaspoon vanilla extract
¼ cup flour stirred with
½ teaspoon baking powder
1 pint (about 2 cups) fresh blueberries

1. Preheat the oven to 350°F; grease a 9 × 9-inch baking pan.

2. Make the bottom layer: In a large bowl, cream the butter, sugar, and grated lemon rind. Gradually add the flour mixture, blending well after each addition. Press the dough evenly onto the bottom of the prepared baking pan. Use a fork to prick the bottom all over. Bake for 13 to 14 minutes, until the edges are lightly browned and the top is dry. Set aside on a wire rack to cool slightly.

3. Make the topping: In a large bowl, cream the cream cheese and sugar. Add the eggs and vanilla and beat again. Add the flour mixture and blend well. Spread the mixture evenly over the baked bottom layer. Sprinkle the blueberries in an even layer on the cream cheese mixture.

4. Bake for 27 to 30 minutes, until the top is golden and a toothpick inserted in the center of the custard topping comes out clean. Place the pan on a wire rack to cool. Cut into 25 squares (5 squares by 5 squares).

WELCOME TO THE NEIGHBORHOOD

It's a time-honored tradition to offer a hearty welcome to the newest member of the neighborhood, the block, the apartment building, or the family—with a delicious gift of homemade cookies. Deliver the gift on a platter or tray of your own, so the newcomer will have a good reason to return your visit, to return your platter. Choose cookies that are standard favorites (shortbread, chocolate cookies, oatmeal chocolate chip cookies, sugar cookies), or bake a batch of rolled cookies in an appropriate shape: booties for a new baby, hearts for a new fiancée, little houses for a new neighbor.

✳

BEACH PARTY PECAN SANDIES

Makes about 3 1/2 dozen cookies

Five ingredients and a simple technique produce a wonderful cookie. Do your baking in the cool of the morning, then pack up your cookies and head for the beach.

> 1 cup (2 sticks) unsalted butter, at room temperature
> 2/3 cup packed light brown sugar
> 1 egg
> 2 cups flour stirred with 1/4 teaspoon salt
> 3/4 cup finely chopped pecans

1. Preheat the oven to 375°F; have ready 1 or 2 ungreased baking sheets.

2. In a large bowl, cream the butter and brown sugar. Add the egg and beat well. Gradually add the flour mixture, blending well after each addition. Stir in the chopped pecans.

3. Drop the dough by level tablespoons, 2 inches apart, onto the ungreased baking sheet. Flatten each drop to 1/4 inch thick, using the flour-dusted bottom of a glass.

4. Bake for 8 to 9 minutes, until the edges are lightly browned. The texture of a cooled cookie will be slightly crumbly and melt-in-your-mouth. Let the cookies cool for 1 or 2 minutes on the baking sheet, then transfer to wire racks to finish cooling.

August

BE GOOD TO yourself on hot summer days. When you need a treat, try No-Bake, Too-Hot-to-Cook Chocolate Cookies that keep kitchen heat to a minimum. Or bake early in the morning when the air is still cool: Fresh Peach Squares make wonderful use of those juicy fresh peaches from the farmers' market, and Mint Cream Sandwiches are simple to prepare and offer a cool taste of peppermint. For a real indulgence, bake a pan of Thin Blondies and tote them along to the nearest swimming pool.

NO-BAKE, TOO-HOT-TO-COOK
CHOCOLATE COOKIES

Makes 40 cookies

When you're longing for a sweet treat but the summer heat makes it impossible even to think of turning on the oven, try these amazing little cookies. A few minutes on a burner are all the cooking they require, and they'll definitely satisfy.

½ cup (1 stick) unsalted butter
1 cup packed light brown sugar
¼ cup heavy cream
2 ounces semisweet chocolate, chopped
1 teaspoon vanilla extract
1½ cups chopped pecans
2 cups graham cracker crumbs
⅛ teaspoon salt

1. In a large heavy saucepan over low heat, melt the butter with the brown sugar, cream, and chopped chocolate, stirring to blend. Remove from the heat and stir in the vanilla. Add the pecans, graham cracker crumbs, and salt and blend well.

2. Pat the mixture evenly into a 9 × 13-inch baking pan. Press a piece of plastic wrap directly onto the surface of the cookies and refrigerate for at least 3 hours. Cut into 40 small squares (5 squares by 8 squares). Remove carefully. Serve at room temperature or chilled, or even frozen.

FRESH PEACH SQUARES

Makes 35 squares

These bar cookies resemble a fruit tart: The crisp, buttery cookie crust is topped with neat rows of sliced fresh peaches and a rich custard. Irresistible.

For the bottom layer:
1½ cups flour
½ cup sugar
Pinch of salt
½ cup (1 stick) cold unsalted butter, cut into pats
5 tablespoons, orange juice

For the topping:
4 medium-size, ripe peaches
1 egg plus 1 egg white
3 tablespoons sugar
½ cup sour cream
½ teaspoon vanilla extract

1. Preheat the oven to 350°F; grease and flour a 9 × 13-inch baking pan.

2. Make the bottom layer: Put the flour, sugar, and salt in the bowl of a food processor and process to combine. Add the butter and process until the mixture looks like cornmeal. Add the orange juice and process again, just until the mixture clumps. Pat the dough evenly over the bottom of the prepared pan, pressing it about ¼ inch up the sides. Use a fork to prick the bottom all over. Bake for 18 to 22 minutes, until lightly browned around the edges. Set aside on a wire rack to cool slightly.

3. Make the topping: Quarter the peaches, discarding the pits and paring away any hard and stringy matter from the centers; cut each quarter

into 4 slices. Overlap the slices on the baked dough, in 4 rows of 16 slices each, as shown.

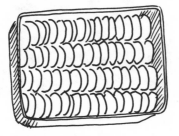

4. In a medium-size bowl, beat together the egg, egg white, sugar, sour cream, and vanilla until well blended. Pour evenly over the peaches.

5. Bake for 18 to 22 minutes, until the edges are well browned, the topping is set, and the peaches can be easily pierced with a fork. Place the pan on a wire rack to cool. Cut into 35 squares (5 squares by 7 squares).

MINT CREAM SANDWICHES

Makes about 2 dozen sandwiches

For mint lovers, here's a crunchy sandwich cookie filled with a lightly minted cream. This is an especially easy dough to work with, and the roll-and-flatten technique for shaping the crisp cookies is super-simple.

For the cookies:
2 cups flour
1½ teaspoons baking powder
½ teaspoon salt
1 egg
½ cup sugar
½ cup heavy cream

For the filling:
¼ cup (½ stick) unsalted butter, at room temperature
1¾ cups confectioners' sugar, sifted
Pinch of salt
¼ teaspoon peppermint extract
½ teaspoon vanilla extract
1½ teaspoons milk

1. Make the cookies: In a medium-size bowl, stir or whisk together the flour, baking powder, and salt. In a large bowl, beat the egg and sugar until thickened. Add the cream and beat again. Gradually add the flour mixture, blending well after each addition. Cover tightly and refrigerate for 30 minutes, or until firm enough to shape.

2. Preheat the oven to 375°F; grease 1 or 2 baking sheets. With flour-dusted palms, shape the dough into ¾- to 1-inch-diameter balls. Place the balls 2 inches apart on the prepared baking sheet. Flatten each ball to ⅛ inch thick, using the flour-dusted bottom of a glass.

3. Bake for 8 to 9 minutes, until the edges are lightly browned. Allow the cookies to cool for 1 or 2 minutes on the baking sheet, then transfer to wire racks to finish cooling.

4. Make the filling: In a large bowl, cream all the filling ingredients until smooth.

5. Make the sandwiches: Turn half the cookies flat side up; divide the filling equally among them and use a small spatula to spread the filling evenly. Top with the remaining cookies, flat sides down. Press the cookies lightly so the sandwiches hold together.

THIN BLONDIES

Makes 48 cookies

The crisp crust on top conceals a rich, chewy, fabulous blondie below—loaded with chocolate chips and toasted pecans. Don't cut them any bigger than recommended; they're luscious but very rich.

1½ cups flour
1 teaspoon baking powder
¼ teaspoon salt
½ cup (1 stick) salted margarine, melted and cooled

1¼ cups packed dark brown sugar
2 eggs
1 cup chopped toasted pecans or walnuts
1 cup semisweet chocolate chips

1. Preheat the oven to 350°F; grease and flour a 10½ × 15½-inch jelly roll pan. In a small bowl, stir or whisk together the flour, baking powder, and salt.

2. In a large bowl, stir together the melted margarine and brown sugar. Add the eggs and beat well. Gradually add the flour mixture, blending well after each addition. Stir in the toasted nuts and chocolate chips.

3. Use a spatula to spread the batter evenly in the prepared pan.

4. Bake for 15 to 18 minutes, until the top is crisp and lightly browned and a toothpick inserted in the center comes out clean. Place the pan on a wire rack and immediately run a knife around the edge of the pan. Carefully score the surface of the blondies in 48 squares (6 squares by 8 squares). Let the blondies cool completely in the pan on a wire rack, then cut apart on the scored lines.

TIP-OF-THE MONTH CLUB:
AUGUST

Serve summer drinks in tall glasses (rinsed, then chilled in the freezer, for a real treat), with appropriate garnishes of mint leaves, berries, chunks of fresh fruit on wooden skewers, thin slices of orange or lemon, or curls of orange or lemon peel. Be sure you have plenty of ice on hand. These drinks make perfect accompaniments to homemade cookies:

- •Lemonade blended with a purée of fresh fruit, such as pineapple, raspberries, or strawberries
- •Orangeade with a squeeze of fresh lime juice
- •Fizzy fruit juice (juice concentrate mixed with seltzer—try grapefruit, cranberry, or tangerine juice)
- •Iced tea spiced with cinnamon and cloves
- •Iced herbal or mint tea
- •Iced tea mixed half-and-half with lemonade or cranberry juice
- •Iced coffee
- •Iced mocha (iced coffee enriched with a little evaporated milk, cocoa powder, and sugar)

✳

September

LEAVES ARE TURNING *and the temperature has dropped just enough to remind us that summer is over. School starts now, and we need some goodies to put in lunch boxes and to serve for afternoon snacks. Harvest Fruit-and-Nut Drop Cookies, Big Sugar Cookies, Double-Crunch Peanut Butter Back-to-School Cookies, and Apple Hermit Squares with Maple Icing are all delicious choices. And for that chocolate craving, Little Chocolate Cookies with Vanilla Glaze will do the trick.*

HARVEST FRUIT-AND-NUT DROP COOKIES

Makes about 4 dozen cookies

Try these golden-brown, craggy nuggets packed with chopped apricots and pecans and a surprise ingredient: raisin bran, which contributes not only the raisins but a rich, grainy flavor and a chewy texture.

1 cup flour	¾ cup packed light brown sugar
1 teaspoon baking powder	3 eggs
¼ teaspoon salt	¼ cup orange juice
3 cups raisin bran cereal	2 teaspoons grated orange rind
¾ cup (1½ sticks) salted margarine, at room temperature	½ cup chopped dried apricots
	¾ cup chopped walnuts or pecans

1. Preheat the oven to 350°F; grease and flour 1 or 2 baking sheets. In a medium-size bowl, stir together the flour, baking powder, salt, and raisin bran.

2. In a large bowl, cream the margarine and brown sugar. Add the eggs, orange juice, and grated orange rind and beat well. Gradually stir in the flour mixture *by hand*, blending well after each addition. Stir in the apricots and nuts.

3. Drop the dough by level tablespoons, 1½ inches apart, onto the prepared baking sheet.

4. Bake for 12 to 13 minutes, until firm to the touch and lightly browned. Let the cookies cool for 1 or 2 minutes on the baking sheet, then transfer to wire racks to finish cooling.

AN ALBUM OF COOKIE RECIPES

Favorite family recipes have a distressing tendency to disappear, but with a little effort you can capture them forever and have a beautiful keepsake to boot.

For starters, it's best to focus on a single topic, such as baking or cookies. Call or write to all your relatives and ask them to send you whatever treasures they have tucked away—Grandmother's Raisin Cookies, Great-Aunt Emma's Chocolate Jumbles, Uncle Harry's Favorite Lemon Wafers, and so on. Ask them to tell you the history of each recipe, or perhaps a story about how the recipe came into the family or why it's such a favorite.

When you've got a good collection, buy a small, pretty album and type up the recipes on pieces of paper or note cards that fit nicely on the pages of the album. Glue the recipes into the album, and write the historical details below the recipe. Don't forget to include your own favorite recipes, too.

BIG SUGAR COOKIES

Makes about 4 dozen cookies

Not your usual thin, crisp variety of sugar cookies—these are large, tender, cakelike cookies with a light lemon flavor and a pretty sprinkling of colored sugar on top. Old-fashioned, and very satisfying. Note that you'll need a 3-inch-diameter round cookie cutter.

4½ cups flour	2 cups sugar
2 teaspoons baking powder	2 eggs
1 teaspoon baking soda	1 teaspoon vanilla extract
½ teaspoon salt	2 teaspoons grated lemon rind
1¼ cups (2½ sticks) unsalted	1 cup buttermilk
butter, at room temperature	Colored sugar for decoration

1. In a large bowl, stir or whisk together the flour, baking powder, baking soda, and salt.

2. In another large bowl, cream the butter and sugar. Add the eggs, vanilla, and grated lemon rind and beat well. Add the flour mixture and buttermilk alternately, in 3 parts, blending well after each addition. The dough will be sticky. Divide the dough into 3 pieces, wrap each piece in plastic, and flatten to about ½ inch thick. Refrigerate for 1 hour, or until firm enough to roll; if you like, speed the process by freezing the dough for a short while.

3. Preheat the oven to 375°F; have ready 2 or more greased baking sheets. Generously dust a work surface and rolling pin with flour. Roll out 1 package of dough to a little less than ¼ inch thick. Cut with a 3-inch-

diameter round cookie cutter. Use a spatula or pancake turner to place the cookies 1½ inches apart on one of the baking sheets. Sprinkle lightly with colored sugar. Gather up and refrigerate the excess dough for rerolling.

Repeat this process with the remaining pieces of dough.

4. Bake for 11 to 12 minutes, until tan on top and lightly browned at the edges. Immediately transfer the cookies to wire racks to cool.

TIP-OF-THE MONTH CLUB:

SEPTEMBER

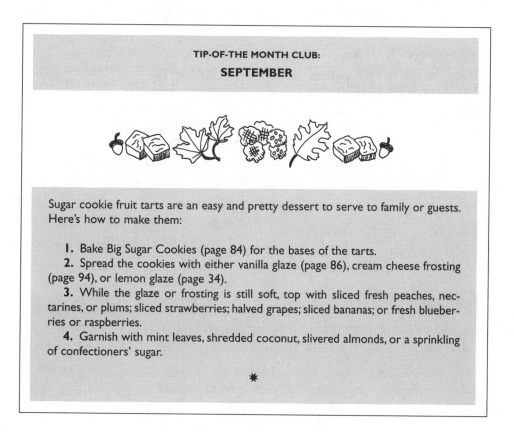

Sugar cookie fruit tarts are an easy and pretty dessert to serve to family or guests. Here's how to make them:

1. Bake Big Sugar Cookies (page 84) for the bases of the tarts.

2. Spread the cookies with either vanilla glaze (page 86), cream cheese frosting (page 94), or lemon glaze (page 34).

3. While the glaze or frosting is still soft, top with sliced fresh peaches, nectarines, or plums; sliced strawberries; halved grapes; sliced bananas; or fresh blueberries or raspberries.

4. Garnish with mint leaves, shredded coconut, slivered almonds, or a sprinkling of confectioners' sugar.

✳

LITTLE CHOCOLATE COOKIES
WITH VANILLA GLAZE

Makes about 8 dozen small cookies

*Light and tender drop cookies with crisp edges and a creamy vanilla glaze.
You could eat a dozen or two. Nice for dessert when you're having company.*

For the glaze:
2 cups confectioners' sugar
5½ tablespoons heavy cream
1 teaspoon vanilla extract
Pinch of salt

For the cookies:
1½ cups flour
⅓ cup cocoa powder
1 teaspoon baking powder
¼ teaspoon baking soda
½ teaspoon salt
¾ cup (1½ sticks) unsalted butter,
   at room temperature
1 cup sugar
2 eggs
1 teaspoon vanilla extract
½ cup sour cream

1. Make the glaze: In a medium-size bowl, beat the confectioners' sugar and cream until smooth. Beat in the vanilla and salt. Cover with plastic wrap pressed directly onto the glaze, to prevent a crust from forming. Set aside.

2. Preheat the oven to 375°F; grease 1 or 2 baking sheets. In a small bowl, stir or whisk together the flour, cocoa, baking powder, baking soda, and salt.

3. In a large bowl, cream the butter and sugar. Add the eggs and vanilla and beat again. Add the flour mixture and sour cream alternately, in 3 parts, blending well after each addition.

4. Drop the dough by teaspoons, 1½ inches apart, onto the prepared baking sheet.

5. Bake for 9 to 10 minutes, until the edges are crisp. They may appear slightly soft; a cooled cookie will be tender but completely cooked. Let the cookies cool on the baking sheet for 1 or 2 minutes, then transfer to wire racks. While the cookies are still very warm (but not hot), spread a scant ½ teaspoon of glaze on each one. Let the cookies finish cooling on the racks; the glaze will firm up as the cookies cool.

DOUBLE-CRUNCH PEANUT BUTTER BACK-TO-SCHOOL COOKIES

Makes about 7 dozen cookies

These are the best peanut butter cookies I've ever tasted—rich and buttery and crisp, made with both crunchy peanut butter and chopped peanuts. As you'd expect, they have lovely rough edges, with the traditional crisscross pattern on top.

2 cups flour
½ teaspoon baking soda
¼ teaspoon salt
10 tablespoons (1 stick plus 2 tablespoons) unsalted
   butter, at room temperature
⅔ cup sugar
⅔ cup packed light brown sugar
1 egg
½ teaspoon vanilla extract
⅔ cup crunchy peanut butter
¾ cup chopped unsalted roasted peanuts

1. Preheat the oven to 350°F; grease 1 or 2 baking sheets. In a small bowl, stir or whisk together the flour, baking soda, and salt.

2. In a large bowl, cream the butter, sugar, and brown sugar. Add the egg and vanilla and beat well. Add the peanut butter and beat again.

Gradually add the flour mixture, blending well after each addition. Stir in the chopped peanuts.

3. Press and shape the dough into 1-inch-diameter balls; the dough is a bit crumbly, so don't try to roll it between your palms. Place the balls 2 inches apart on the prepared baking sheet. Use the flour-dusted tines of a fork to flatten each cookie to a little less than ¼ inch thick, making the traditional crisscross lines on the top. The edges should look rough and uneven; don't try to smooth them out.

4. Bake for 9 to 11 minutes, until lightly browned on the edges. Allow the cookies to cool for 3 to 4 minutes on the baking sheet, then transfer to wire racks to finish cooling.

APPLE HERMIT SQUARES
WITH MAPLE ICING

Makes 40 squares

These cakelike bar cookies are adapted from traditional hermit cookies (which are spicy and full of chopped fruits and nuts) and frosted generously with real maple syrup icing.

2½ cups flour
1 teaspoon baking powder
½ teaspoon baking soda
¼ teaspoon salt
½ teaspoon cinnamon
¼ teaspoon nutmeg
1 medium-size cooking apple,
   such as Jonathan, Rome Beauty,
   Ida Red, or Baldwin
¾ cup (1½ sticks) salted margarine,
   at room temperature
1 cup packed light brown sugar
2 eggs
1 teaspoon vanilla extract
½ cup milk
½ cup golden raisins
½ cup chopped pecans

For the icing:
3 tablespoons unsalted butter,
   melted and cooled
2 cups confectioners' sugar, sifted
¼ cup maple syrup
½ teaspoon vanilla extract
⅛ teaspoon salt

1. Preheat the oven to 375°F; grease and flour a 10½ × 15½-inch baking pan. In a medium-size bowl, stir or whisk together the flour, baking powder, baking soda, salt, and spices. Peel, quarter, and core the apple, making sure to remove all the seeds and hard matter; chop into pea-size bits (about 1½ cups).

2. In a large bowl, cream the margarine and brown sugar. Add the eggs and vanilla and beat until well blended. Add the flour mixture and milk alternately, in 3 parts, blending well after each addition. Stir in the raisins, pecans, and chopped apples.

3. Using a small spatula, spread the batter evenly in the prepared pan.

4. Bake for 22 to 25 minutes, until the top is dry and lightly browned and a toothpick inserted in the center comes out clean. Let the cookies cool in the pan until warm.

5. Make the icing: Combine the ingredients in a large bowl and beat until smooth. Using a small spatula dipped in hot water, spread the icing evenly on the warm (not hot) cookies. Let the icing set, then cut into 40 squares (5 squares by 8 squares).

October

GOLDEN LIGHT, *blue skies, a canopy of brightly colored leaves—it's full autumn, and we suddenly have a yen for the rich flavors that complement October's invigorating air. Pumpkin Spice Bars with Cream Cheese Frosting and Golden Raisin Cookies will definitely satisfy the appetite, and so will crunchy brown sugar Butterscotch Icebox Cookies and chewy almond Pignoli Cookies.*

PUMPKIN SPICE BARS
WITH CREAM CHEESE FROSTING

Makes 32 bars

Here's a thin, slightly chewy bar laced with chopped golden raisins and walnuts, topped with a rich cream cheese frosting. There's a good flavor of pumpkin and spices, just like pumpkin pie. Great for munching on a cool October afternoon.

1¾ cups flour
1 teaspoon baking powder
¼ teaspoon salt
1 teaspoon cinnamon
½ teaspoon nutmeg
¼ teaspoon ground ginger
½ cup (1 stick) salted margarine, at
  room temperature
1¼ cups packed light brown sugar
1 egg
1⅓ cups canned pumpkin purée
1 cup coarsely chopped golden raisins
1 cup finely chopped walnuts

For the frosting:
3 ounces cream cheese, at room
  temperature
2 cups confectioners' sugar, sifted
1 teaspoon vanilla extract
Pinch of salt
2 tablespoons milk

1. Preheat the oven to 375°F; grease and flour a 10½ × 15½-inch jelly roll pan. In a small bowl, stir or whisk together the flour, baking powder, salt, and spices.

2. In a large bowl, cream the margarine and brown sugar. Add the egg and beat again. Add the flour mixture and pumpkin purée alternately, in 3 parts, blending well after each addition. Stir in the chopped raisins and walnuts.

3. Spread the batter evenly in the prepared pan.

4. Bake for 20 to 22 minutes, until the edges are pulling away from the pan and a toothpick inserted in the center of the pan comes out clean. Place the pan on a wire rack and run a knife around the edge. Allow to cool in the pan.

5. Make the frosting: In a large bowl, beat the cream cheese until smooth. Gradually beat in half of the confectioners' sugar. Add the vanilla, salt, and milk and beat again. Beat in the remaining confectioners' sugar.

6. Frost evenly, then cut into 32 bars (4 bars by 8 bars), wiping the knife between cuts.

BUTTERSCOTCH ICEBOX COOKIES

Makes about 7 ½ dozen cookies

This recipe makes a lot of cookies if you slice and bake both logs at once. Instead, slice and bake one log today and leave one log in the freezer for unexpected guests or for that midnight cookie craving.

3 cups flour
1 teaspoon baking powder
½ teaspoon salt
½ cup (1 stick) unsalted butter,
   at room temperature
2 cups packed light brown sugar
2 eggs
1 teaspoon vanilla extract

1. In a medium-size bowl, stir or whisk together the flour, baking powder, and salt.

2. In a large bowl, cream the butter and brown sugar as best you can; the mixture will be grainy, but be sure all the brown sugar lumps are broken up. Add the eggs and vanilla and beat well. Gradually add the flour mixture, blending well after each addition.

3. Divide the dough in half and place each half on a piece of plastic wrap. Using the plastic to help, shape each half into a smooth log about 2 inches in diameter. Wrap snugly in the plastic and refrigerate overnight, turning and smoothing the logs occasionally to maintain the cylindrical shape.

4. Preheat the oven to 400°F; grease 1 or 2 baking sheets. Unwrap 1 log of dough and use a sharp knife to cut it into ⅛-inch-thick slices. Place the slices 1 inch apart on the prepared baking sheet.

Repeat with the second log or reserve it for future use.

5. If you like very crisp cookies, bake for 8 to 9 minutes, until the tops are golden and the edges are lightly browned. If you prefer cookies that are chewy in the center, bake for 7 to 8 minutes and don't let the edges brown. In either case, immediately transfer the cookies to wire racks to cool.

TIP-OF-THE-MONTH CLUB:
OCTOBER

The ground spices you'll use most often in cookie baking are cinnamon, ginger, nutmeg, allspice, and cloves. Of course you want them to be fresh and aromatic, not stale or musty. Unfortunately, ground spices tend to lose their punch rather quickly, so buy these in small quantities, store them in a cool, dark place, and discard after about six months. If you hate the thought of throwing your spices away, buy with a buddy. Split the spice and the price—you won't spend a bundle and you won't have so much to toss out.

✳

GOLDEN RAISIN COOKIES

Makes about 7 dozen small cookies

Bite-size, pop-in-your-mouth drop cookies with a light lemon flavor and a generous helping of golden raisins in the dough. Easy to put together anytime you want a batch of homemade goodies.

2 cups flour
1 teaspoon baking powder
½ teaspoon salt
¾ cup (1½ sticks) unsalted butter,
   at room temperature

¾ cup sugar
1 egg
¼ cup milk
1 teaspoon grated lemon rind
1 cup golden raisins

1. Preheat the oven to 400°F; grease 1 or 2 baking sheets. In a medium-size bowl, stir or whisk together the flour, baking powder, and salt.

2. In a large bowl, cream the butter and sugar. Add the egg, milk, and grated lemon rind and beat well. Gradually add the flour mixture, blending well after each addition. Stir in the raisins.

3. Drop the dough by rounded teaspoons, 2 inches apart, onto the prepared baking sheet. With a dampened fingertip, flatten each cookie slightly.

4. Bake for 8 to 9 minutes, until the edges are golden brown. Let the cookies cool for 1 or 2 minutes on the baking sheet, then transfer to wire racks to finish cooling.

PIGNOLI COOKIES

Makes about 4 1/2 dozen cookies

For serious almond lovers—a traditional Italian cookie that's almost like marzipan, studded with lots of pine nuts that toast during baking. Pignoli cookies are deliciously crisp on the outside, chewy on the inside. This version is made with the help of your food processor.

14 ounces (two 7-ounce tubes) commercial pure
   almond paste (not marzipan)
1 cup sugar
1/2 cup sifted confectioners' sugar
Pinch of salt
3 egg whites
2 1/2 cups pignolis (pine nuts)

1. Preheat the oven to 325°F; line 2 baking sheets with baking parchment. *Tip:* Dampen the baking sheet so the parchment will adhere easily.

2. Crumble the almond paste into a food processor. Add the sugar, confectioners' sugar, salt, and egg whites and process until well blended and smooth. Be sure to scrape down the bowl several times. The mixture will be very sticky. Transfer to a bowl, cover with plastic, and refrigerate for 1 hour.

3. With moistened palms, shape the dough into 1-inch-diameter balls; place the balls on a piece of waxed paper. Roll each ball in pignolis,

then roll between your palms again to embed the nuts firmly in the dough. Place the balls about 2 inches apart on the baking sheets. Flatten each ball slightly.

4. Bake for 20 minutes, until both the cookies and the pignolis are lightly browned. Let the cookies cool completely on the parchment, then lift them off and let them dry on wire racks for 1 hour before serving or storing.

November

THERE'S PLENTY to be thankful for in November: Oatmeal Chocolate Chip Cookies and Crisp Orange Cookies, too. For festive holiday dinners, serve your guests meltingly delicious Hazelnut Shortbread and pretty Cranberry-Walnut Squares with Crumb Topping.

OATMEAL CHOCOLATE CHIP COOKIES

Makes about 4 dozen cookies

*Instead of the usual raisins, these oatmeal cookies contain chocolate chips—
a really delicious variation. Properly crunchy on the outside, moist and chewy
on the inside. If you like, add chopped walnuts or pecans.*

1 cup flour
2¼ cups quick (1-minute) oatmeal, uncooked
½ teaspoon baking soda
¼ teaspoon salt
¾ cup (1½ sticks) salted margarine, at room
   temperature
½ cup sugar
½ cup packed light brown sugar
1 egg
¼ cup milk
1 teaspoon vanilla extract
1 cup semisweet chocolate chips
Chopped walnuts or pecans (optional)

1. Preheat the oven to 350°F; grease 1 or 2 baking sheets. In a
medium-size bowl, stir or whisk together the flour, oatmeal, baking soda,
and salt.

2. In a large bowl, cream the margarine, sugar, and brown sugar. Add
the egg, milk, and vanilla and beat again. Gradually add the flour mixture,
blending well after each addition. Stir in the chocolate chips.

3. Drop the dough by level tablespoons, 2 inches apart, onto the prepared baking sheet.

4. Bake for 12 to 13 minutes, until lightly browned and crisp on the edges and tops. Let the cookies cool for 1 minute on the baking sheet, then transfer to wire racks to finish cooling.

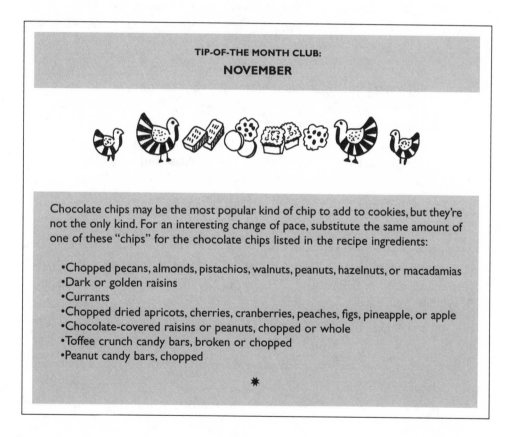

TIP-OF-THE MONTH CLUB:
NOVEMBER

Chocolate chips may be the most popular kind of chip to add to cookies, but they're not the only kind. For an interesting change of pace, substitute the same amount of one of these "chips" for the chocolate chips listed in the recipe ingredients:

- Chopped pecans, almonds, pistachios, walnuts, peanuts, hazelnuts, or macadamias
- Dark or golden raisins
- Currants
- Chopped dried apricots, cherries, cranberries, peaches, figs, pineapple, or apple
- Chocolate-covered raisins or peanuts, chopped or whole
- Toffee crunch candy bars, broken or chopped
- Peanut candy bars, chopped

HAZELNUT SHORTBREAD

Makes 36 bars

Shortbread is an amazing cookie—so few ingredients to achieve such an out-standing result, tender and melting. And so simple to make, too. This one has the bonus of a rich taste of hazelnuts. Tip: Shortbread keeps extremely well in the freezer in an airtight plastic container.

1 cup (2 sticks) unsalted butter, at room temperature
½ cup superfine sugar
1 teaspoon vanilla extract
½ cup toasted, finely chopped skinned hazelnuts (see
   page 61 for information on how to toast and skin
   hazelnuts)
2 cups flour stirred with ⅛ teaspoon salt

1. In a large bowl, cream the butter, sugar, and vanilla. Stir the chopped hazelnuts into the flour mixture. Gradually add the flour mixture to the butter mixture, blending well after each addition, to make a soft dough.

2. With flour-dusted hands, place the dough on an ungreased baking sheet and pat it out to an 8 × 9-inch rectangle. Use the edge of a ruler to score the dough in 1 × 2-inch bars, as shown. Use a fork to prick each bar 3 or 4 times. Cover tightly with plastic wrap and refrigerate for 1 hour, or until firm.

3. Preheat the oven to 350°F; have ready an additional ungreased

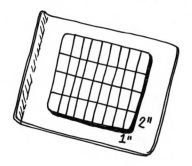

baking sheet. Cut the chilled dough into bars, following the scored lines, and use a spatula to place them 1 inch apart on the baking sheets.

4. If possible, bake only 1 sheet at a time in the center of the oven for 18 to 20 minutes, until lightly colored. If necessary, bake both sheets at the same time, 1 sheet on the middle shelf and 1 on the shelf above, for 12 minutes; then reverse the positions of the 2 baking sheets in the oven and bake for 6 to 8 minutes longer. Do not overbake; the bars should not brown. Let the bars cool on the baking sheet for 2 or 3 minutes, then carefully transfer to wire racks to finish cooling.

CRISP ORANGE COOKIES

Makes about 5 1/2 dozen cookies

This easy-to-roll dough makes a thin, crisp cookie with a light orange flavor. Good alone, with fruit, or made into sandwiches—fill with vanilla glaze (page 86) or cream cheese frosting (page 94).

2½ cups flour
2 teaspoons baking powder
¼ teaspoon salt
¼ cup (½ stick) unsalted butter, at room temperature
1 cup sugar
4 egg yolks
2 tablespoons orange juice
1 teaspoon grated orange rind

1. Preheat the oven to 375°F; grease 1 or 2 baking sheets. In a medium-size bowl, stir or whisk together the flour, baking powder, and salt.

2. In a large bowl, blend the butter and sugar; the mixture will be grainy. Add the egg yolks, orange juice, and grated rind and beat for several minutes, until pale and light. Gradually add the flour mixture, blending well after each addition; the dough will be stiff, so blend the last addition of flour by hand.

3. Divide the dough in half. Dust your work surface and rolling pin with flour. Roll out 1 piece of dough to about ⅛ inch thick. Cut with a

2-inch-diameter round cookie cutter or a drinking glass. Place the cookies 1 inch apart on the prepared baking sheet. Gather up the excess dough for rerolling.

Repeat this process with the second piece of dough.

4. Bake for 10 to 11 minutes, until the edges are browned. Immediately transfer the cookies to wire racks to cool.

CRANBERRY-WALNUT SQUARES
WITH CRUMB TOPPING

Makes 25 squares

Here's a tender cookie crust spread with a sweet-tart cranberry conserve, sprinkled with walnut crumb topping. Each small square is like a rich jam bar.

For the filling:
1 cup dried cranberries, coarsely
  chopped
½ cup orange juice
1 tablespoon fresh lemon juice
½ cup sugar
1 tablespoon unsalted butter
1 tablespoon flour
Pinch of salt

For the bottom layer:
1¼ cups flour
1 teaspoon baking powder
½ teaspoon salt

½ cup (1 stick) unsalted butter, at
  room temperature
¼ cup packed light brown sugar
2 egg yolks
1 teaspoon vanilla extract

For the crumb topping:
6 tablespoons flour
¼ cup sugar
⅛ teaspoon salt
3 tablespoons cold unsalted butter,
  cut into pats
¼ cup chopped walnuts

1. Preheat the oven to 350°F; grease a 9 × 9-inch baking pan.
2. Make the filling: In a heavy saucepan over medium heat, stir together all the filling ingredients. Bring to a boil, reduce the heat, and simmer, stirring constantly, for 5 minutes, until thick. Set aside to cool.

3. Make the bottom layer: In a small bowl, stir or whisk together the flour, baking powder, and salt. In a large bowl, cream the butter and brown sugar. Add the egg yolks and vanilla and beat again. Gradually add the flour mixture, blending well after each addition. With moistened fingers, pat the dough evenly into the prepared pan, pressing it up the sides about 1/4 inch.

4. Make the crumb topping: Put the flour, sugar, salt, and butter in a food processor and pulse until the mixture is crumbly; do not overprocess. Add the nuts and pulse once or twice to blend.

5. Spread the cooled filling evenly over the bottom layer. Sprinkle the crumb topping evenly over the filling.

6. Bake for 25 to 30 minutes, until the bottom layer is nicely browned around the edges and the crumb topping is lightly browned. Place the pan on a wire rack, run a knife around the edges to loosen the dough, then allow to cool completely. Cut into 25 squares (5 squares by 5 squares).

December

THIS IS THE MONTH to pull out all the stops and fill the house with the delicious smell of homemade cookies. Brightly colored Rainbow Christmas Stars and pink-and-white Candy Cane Cookies will send your kids into raptures. Decorate your tree and wreaths with Gingerbread Cookie Ornaments. Offer your guests beautifully arranged trays of Traditional Almond Spritz Cookies and Tiny Turnovers with Fig Filling. And the perfect finishing touch to any holiday meal— Chocolate-Bourbon Truffles.

RAINBOW CHRISTMAS STARS

Makes about 4 dozen cookies

These stars are made with six different colors of dough—and they are stunning to behold. Use paste or gel food coloring for truly brilliant colors; if you're careful not to overbake the cookies, the colors will stay clear and bright. Note that you'll need a 2½- to 3-inch star-shaped cookie cutter.

> 4½ cups flour
> 1½ teaspoons baking powder
> ½ teaspoon salt
> 1½ cups (3 sticks) unsalted butter, at room temperature
> 1½ cups sugar
> 2 eggs
> 2 teaspoons vanilla extract
> Food coloring (gel or paste)

1. In a large bowl, stir or whisk together the flour, baking powder, and salt.

2. In another large bowl, cream the butter and sugar. Add the eggs and vanilla and beat again. Gradually add the flour mixture, blending well after each addition. Divide the dough into 6 approximately equal pieces.

3. To color the dough, you'll need either gel or paste food coloring. Put 1 piece of dough in each of 5 small bowls. To each, add a different coloring and blend well to make 5 different colors; a good range might include yellow, red, green, medium blue, and orange or lavender. Leave the sixth piece of dough uncolored. Divide each piece of dough (5 colored

and 1 uncolored) into thirds, wrap each piece in plastic, and refrigerate for 2 hours, or until firm.

4. Preheat the oven to 375°F; grease 1 or 2 baking sheets. Dust a work surface and rolling pin with flour. To make the first batch of cookies, take out 1 package of each color and 1 package of uncolored dough. Break off marble-size pieces of dough and arrange them, *touching* each other on the floured surface, in a colorful random pattern. Gently press the dough flat, dust with flour, and then carefully roll out to a ⅛-inch-thick multicolored sheet of dough. Cut with a 2½- to 3-inch star-shaped cookie cutter. The excess dough *cannot* be rerolled (the colors become muddy and gray), so be sure to cut as many cookies as possible.

Use a spatula or pancake turner to place the cookies 1 inch apart on the prepared baking sheet. Discard the excess dough.

Repeat this process 2 more times, using the remaining dough.

5. Bake for 9 to 10 minutes, until the edges are golden. Be careful not to overbake the cookies, or the colors will become too brown. Let the cookies cool for 1 or 2 minutes on the baking sheet, then transfer to wire racks to finish cooling.

GINGERBREAD COOKIE ORNAMENTS

Makes about 3 1/2 dozen cookies

This delicious gingerbread dough is perfect for making ornaments to hang on your Christmas tree or wreath. You'll need a plastic straw or a chopstick for making holes; you'll also need narrow ribbon, cord, or yarn for hanging the cookie ornaments. If you like, use ready-made icing and your own tips to pipe decorations onto the cookies.

3 to 3 1/4 cups flour
1 teaspoon baking soda
1/2 teaspoon salt
1 teaspoon cinnamon
1/2 teaspoon ground ginger
1/4 teaspoon ground cloves
1/2 cup (1 stick) unsalted butter,
   at room temperature

1/2 cup packed dark brown sugar
1/2 cup unsulphured molasses
   (not blackstrap)
1 egg
2 teaspoons cider vinegar

1. In a small bowl, stir or whisk together 2½ cups of the flour and the baking soda, salt, and spices.

2. In a large bowl, cream the butter and brown sugar. Add the molasses and beat until well blended. Add the egg and vinegar and beat again. Gradually add the flour mixture, blending well after each addition. Gradually stir in another ½ cup flour. The dough should be firm but sticky, neither dry nor soft; if necessary, blend in some or all of the remaining ¼ cup flour. Divide the dough in half, shape each piece into an inch-thick disk, and wrap each disk in plastic. Refrigerate for 2 hours, or until firm enough to roll.

3. Preheat the oven to 350°F; grease 1 or 2 baking sheets. Dust a work surface and rolling pin with flour. Roll out 1 piece of dough to ⅛ inch thick. Cut with your favorite Christmas cookie cutters—gingerbread boy and girl, Santa, bell, angel, or others. Use a spatula or pancake turner to place the cookies 1 inch apart on the prepared baking sheet. Gather up the excess dough for rerolling.

Repeat this process with the remaining dough.

4. Use either a plastic drinking straw or the end of a chopstick to make a ¼-inch hole near the top of each cookie.

5. Bake for 10 to 12 minutes, until the edges are browned; a few of the holes will close up, but most will remain open. Let the cookies cool on the baking sheet for 1 minute, then transfer to wire racks to finish cooling.

6. To hang the cookie ornaments, thread short lengths of narrow ribbon, cord, or yarn through the holes and tie to the Christmas tree.

TRADITIONAL ALMOND SPRITZ COOKIES

Makes about 8 1/2 dozen small cookies

If you've never made spritz cookies before, it may take you a few tries to get the hang of using a cookie press—but these delicate, wonderful cookies are worth the effort. Tip: I prefer not to decorate them, but if you like, drizzle with thin chocolate glaze.

1 egg plus 1 egg yolk, at room
  temperature
¾ cup superfine sugar
¼ cup ground, blanched raw
  almonds
1 teaspoon vanilla extract
½ teaspoon almond extract
2 cups flour stirred with
  ¼ teaspoon salt
1 cup (2 sticks) unsalted butter,
  melted and cooled

For the glaze (optional):
2 ounces semisweet chocolate,
  chopped
5 teaspoons water
1 teaspoon vegetable oil

1. In a large bowl, beat the egg, egg yolk, and sugar until pale yellow, smooth, and thick. Beat in the ground almonds, vanilla, and almond extract. Add the flour mixture and melted butter alternately, in 3 parts, blending well after each addition. Cover the dough with plastic wrap and refrigerate for 30 minutes; don't chill the dough any more than 30 minutes or it will become too stiff to pass through the cookie press.

2. Preheat the oven to 350°F; grease 1 or 2 baking sheets. Have ready a cookie press fitted with your choice of disk, such as a flower, wreath, or Christmas tree. Pack dough into the cookie press. Press the dough onto the prepared baking sheet, leaving 1½ inches between cookies.

3. Bake for 11 to 13 minutes, until the cookies are slightly browned around the edges. Do not overbake. Immediately transfer to wire racks to cool.

4. To make the glaze, stir the ingredients together in a heavy saucepan over low heat until smooth. Arrange the cooled cookies close together on the wire rack. Dip a small wire whisk into the chocolate and swing it back and forth over the cookies in two different directions to make a lattice pattern. Let the chocolate harden.

TIP-OF-THE-MONTH CLUB:
DECEMBER

It's great fun to add a little color to any pale cookie dough or to a white glaze, icing, or frosting. Once upon a time you could do this only with liquid food coloring added by drops from little glass or plastic bottles. Now you have more choices: Paste colors in small jars are highly concentrated; use a toothpick to transfer the color from the jar to your dough or icing, then mix thoroughly. Even better than paste are gel colors in plastic bottles with built-in droppers; simply squeeze out as much color as you need and mix well.

✳

CHOCOLATE-BOURBON TRUFFLES

Makes about 7 1/2 dozen truffles

These little balls of rich chocolate, vanilla cookie crumbs, and pecans are spiked with a hearty nip of bourbon. There's no baking involved; instead, the dough is chilled overnight, then the truffles are shaped and allowed to ripen. Be sure to make the truffles several days before needed.

6 ounces high-quality semisweet chocolate (such as Callebaut, Lindt, Valrhona, or Ghirardelli), chopped
1/4 cup sugar
3 tablespoons light corn syrup
1/2 cup bourbon
1/4 cup water

2 1/2 cups finely crushed vanilla cookie crumbs (such as crumbs made from Nabisco Nilla wafers)
1/2 cup toasted finely chopped pecans
2 tablespoons sugar stirred with 1 tablespoon cocoa powder

1. In a heavy saucepan over low heat, melt the chocolate, sugar, corn syrup, bourbon, and water together, stirring until smooth and well combined. Transfer to a large bowl.

2. Stir in the cookie crumbs and chopped nuts. Let the mixture stand at room temperature for 30 minutes. Transfer to a plastic container, cover tightly, and refrigerate overnight to allow the mixture to thicken and firm up.

3. With moistened palms, shape the chilled dough into balls a little less than 1 inch in diameter. Roll each ball in the sugar-cocoa mixture.

Arrange the truffles in layers in an airtight container, separating the layers with waxed paper. Refrigerate the truffles and allow them to age for several days before serving.

DECORATING WITH CHRISTMAS COOKIES

Cookies on the mantel, on a window ledge, on a wreath, and on the Christmas tree—cookies all around the holiday house.

✳

TINY TURNOVERS WITH FIG FILLING

Makes about 3 1/2 dozen turnovers

Guests love these tender little half-moon-shaped cookies—and you'll love how easily you can make the turnover dough in your food processor. Tip: If you don't care for fig filling, use thick preserves or ready-made almond filling.

1 egg yolk
1/3 cup sour cream
1 1/2 cups flour
1/8 teaspoon salt
1/4 cup sugar
3/4 cup (1 1/2 sticks) cold unsalted
    butter, cut into pats

For the filling:
2/3 cup chopped dried figs (cut with
    a serrated knife or snipped with
    scissors)
1/2 cup water
1 tablespoon packed light brown
    sugar
1/2 teaspoon grated orange rind
Pinch of salt
1/4 cup finely chopped raw almonds
    (with or without skins)
1/4 teaspoon almond extract

1. In a small bowl, stir together the egg yolk and sour cream.
2. In the bowl of a food processor, combine the flour, salt, and sugar. Add the pats of butter and process just until the mixture looks like coarse cornmeal. Add the egg mixture and process until a ball of dough forms on top of the blades. Turn out onto a flour-dusted surface and knead several strokes, until the dough is very smooth and pliable. Divide the dough in

half, shape each piece into an inch-thick disk, and wrap each disk in plastic. Refrigerate for 1 hour.

3. Make the fig filling: In a heavy saucepan over low heat, simmer all the ingredients except the almonds and almond extract for 15 minutes, stirring often, until all the water is absorbed and the mixture is like thick jam. Turn off the heat and stir in the almonds and almond extract. Set aside to cool.

4. Preheat the oven to 375°F; have ready 1 or 2 ungreased baking sheets. Dust a work surface and rolling pin with flour. Roll out 1 piece of dough to 1/8 inch thick. Cut with a 2 1/2-inch-diameter round cookie cutter. Use a spatula or pancake turner to place the cookies 1/2 inch apart on the ungreased baking sheet. Gather up the excess dough for rerolling.

Repeat this process with the second piece of dough.

5. Place 1/2 teaspoon of filling in the center of 1 cookie. With a small pastry brush, brush water around the edge of the cookie. Carefully fold the cookie over the filling and seal by pressing the edges together with the tines of a fork as shown. Prick once with the fork.

Repeat this process with all the remaining cookies.

6. Bake for 12 to 13 minutes, until the tops are tan and the edges are lightly browned; the bottoms will be golden brown. Let the cookies cool on the baking sheet for about 1 minute, then transfer to wire racks to finish cooling.

CANDY CANE COOKIES

Makes about 3½ dozen cookies

Crisp and pretty and right in the spirit of the season. There's a fair amount of time involved in making these cookies, but the results are rewarding. And the technique is simple—it's just a matter of rolling bits of dough into ropes and gently twisting them together.

> 3½ cups flour
> 2 teaspoons baking powder
> ½ teaspoon salt
> 1 cup (2 sticks) unsalted butter, at room temperature
> 1¼ cups sugar
> 2 eggs
> 2 teaspoons vanilla extract
> Red food coloring

1. In a medium-size bowl, stir or whisk together the flour, baking powder, and salt.
2. In a large bowl, cream the butter and sugar. Add the eggs and vanilla

and beat again. Gradually add the flour mixture, blending well after each addition. Put half the dough in another bowl and blend in just enough red food coloring to make a deep pink. Flatten each piece of dough into an inch-thick disk and wrap it in plastic; refrigerate for 30 minutes.

3. Preheat the oven to 350°F; grease 1 or 2 baking sheets. Dust your hands and a work surface with flour. Roll a piece of the pink dough into a 1-inch-diameter ball; roll a piece of the white dough into a 1-inch-diameter ball. Roll each ball into a rope about 6 inches long.

Center the white rope over the pink one and spiral them together from the middle to the ends as shown. Press the ends together lightly at each end. Transfer the twist to the baking sheet and shape it into a candy cane.

Repeat this process with all the remaining dough, leaving 1½ inches between cookies. If the dough becomes too soft to work with, chill it again.

4. Bake for 13 to 15 minutes, until very lightly browned on the edges. The cookies will be a little soft on top, but they become crisper as they cool. Let them cool on the baking sheet for 2 minutes, then carefully transfer to wire racks to finish cooling.

MAKING A COOKIE WREATH FOR CHRISTMAS

This festive holiday wreath is simple to make and will look lovely above the mantel or *inside* the front door. Make small Gingerbread Cookie Ornaments (page 114) with holes, and thread the holes with narrow red satin ribbon or red yarn. Tie the cookies to the branches of a ready-made evergreen or grapevine wreath.

✳

Index

kisses
Mocha-Glazed Vanilla Meringue
Kisses, 22–23
kitchen tools
basics, 3–4

Ladyfingers, 26–27
Lemon Teacakes with Lemon Glaze,
34–35
lemonade, 80
Lindt (chocolate brand), 1, 11
Linzer Hearts, 53–55
liquids
measuring, 1–2
measuring cups, 3
Little Chocolate Cookies with Vanilla
Glaze, 86–87

macadamia nut cookies
Aloha Cookies, 63
macaroons
Coconut Macaroons, 44
measuring, 1–2
conversion tables, 27
dry ingredients, 2
flour, 1
liquids, 1–2
measuring cups, 3
measuring spoons, 3
Melt-in-Your-Mouth Cornmeal
Cookies, 60–61

meringue cookies
Mocha-Glazed Vanilla Meringue
Kisses, 22–23
Mexican Wedding Cookies, 62
Mint Cream Sandwiches, 77–78
mixing bowls, 3
Mocha-Glazed Vanilla Meringue
Kisses, 22–23
molasses cookies
Iced Molasses Drops, 10–11
Mom's Favorite Butter Cookies,
48–49

neighborhood welcome, 71
Nestlé's chocolate, 11
No-Bake, Too-Hot-to-Cook
Chocolate Cookies, 74
nut cookies
Almond-Cherry Cups, 24–25
Aloha Cookies, 63
Apple Hermit Squares with Maple
Icing, 90–91
Beach Party Pecan Sandies,
72
Cranberry-Walnut Squares with
Crumb Topping, 108–9
Double-Crunch Peanut Butter
Back-to-School Cookies,
88–89
Glazed Banana-Nut Squares,
45–46